FIRST JOB

FIRST JOB

A New Grad's Guide to Launching Your Business Career

RICHARD FEIN

JOHN WILEY & SONS, INC.

New York • Chichester • Brisbane • Toronto • Singapore

In recognition of the importance of preserving what has been
written, it is a policy of John Wiley & Sons, Inc., to have
books of enduring value published in the United States
printed on acid-free paper, and we exert our best efforts
to that end.

Library of Congress Cataloging-in-Publication Data

Fein, Richard, 1946–
    First job : a new grad's guide to launching your
business career / by Richard Fein.
        p.   cm.
    ISBN 0-471-57457-0 (paper)
    1. Job hunting—United States—Handbooks, manuals, etc.
    2. Résumés (Employment)—Handbooks, manuals, etc.
HF5382.75.U6F45   1992
650.14—dc20   91-46491

Printed in the United States of America

10 9 8 7 6 5 4 3 2 1

Preface

Getting a job is serious business. Getting a job can influence the rest of your life—your sense of satisfaction, your income, even who your friends are.

As you completed each year of high school, you went on to the next year's curriculum. When you finished your sophomore courses in college, you became a junior. As long as you fulfilled certain requirements, you advanced to the next step in your academic career.

Getting a job is not like that: There is no automatic good job awaiting you simply because you did well in college. Life in general is not organized like academic life. No one, obvious step follows implicitly from another. There is a tremendous amount of competition for good professional jobs. In college, if you studied hard and got 100 percent for an exam, you probably got an A. In life beyond college, even an A doesn't guarantee anything. To complicate matters, what is valued as an A in one situation may be only a C+ in another.

This book is designed to help you become well-employed when you graduate from college. I will offer you no slick tricks and nothing hokey. Instead, I will show you what you need to do, and how to do it, to maximize your chances of success.

This book is built around basic job search principles that have been applied by the students I have helped in my 11 years as a college placement director. These principles will be explained, annotated, and illustrated by numerous examples. I will show you how to identify your Positive Characteristics and how to support them with convincing examples. This combination is a key element in your job search success.

To prepare for your job search, you will be getting rid of your useless "baggage," especially your career-wrecking myths. One by one, I will describe and debunk the myths. You will be working smarter if you work without them.

WHAT'S IN THIS BOOK FOR YOU?

I have organized this book so that you can take your job search from awkward start to successful finish. Many texts advocate starting with pen-and-paper self-assessment tests. I do not, for reasons that I explain in the early chapters. Instead, I encourage you to "Ask the Pros"—the single best way to find out about the corporate world *and* yourself. I give you examples of characteristics that are important to typical business jobs and tell you how to research characteristics on your own.

My discussion of résumé writing establishes the principles for you to follow and then gives you *extensive* examples of how to build, draft, redraft, and complete your résumé. I encourage you to focus on your message and support it with examples. You will not find dull "One Day in the Life of a Waiter" résumés in this book. Nor will you find photocopies of "successful résumés"; they would be almost useless to you in writing your own. Instead, you will see how résumés develop, step-by-step, as a basis for your own résumé.

I will tell you when you need cover letters and how to write them. You will also learn why you need an outreach list and how to build one.

In the chapters on interviewing, I will show you how to prepare, what's important, and how to successfully conduct your interview. You will learn my Ten Principles of Interviewing and how to apply them.

I will analyze ten common and ten especially difficult interviewers' questions, with possible responses. You will learn how the question–answer–question cycle works and how you can use it to set up at least part of the agenda at your interview. I will show you mistakes to avoid and approaches to use for success. You will learn how to ask *your questions* at the interview, using my Four Basic Environments, and how to open and close your interview.

One of several special features in this book is the process *after* your initial interview with a particular firm. An extensive discussion of the Site Visit tells you what makes it different from your initial interview and what special preparation you need for success. A chapter on job offers tells you what they mean and how to handle multiple opportunities. A chapter on the Follow-up Visit explains in detail how and why to visit a firm again, *after* it has extended an offer to you. You will learn a no-lose approach to negotiating your starting salary, how to evaluate job offers, and how to "close the loops"—a necessary but often neglected process.

There are no tricks in this book. I urge you to put in effort, not put on a front. Putting in is honest and it works.

THE STEP-BY-STEP APPROACH

In the process of finding a good job, each step proceeds from the previous one. Good research leads to a good résumé, which leads to more interviews, which leads to more job offers. This book is written in the same step-by-step way. The skills and insights you gain from asking the pros will help you to construct a winning résumé, which will win you more interviews. Your preparation of a good résumé message will help your initial interviews, which will result in succeeding at Site Visits and parlaying successful Site Visits into good job offers at the best possible starting salaries. Throughout, frequent reinforcement of key points will connect one stage of the process to another.

This book is designed for you to use on your own or with a group of job-seeking friends. We will follow seven students—composites of actual students I have worked with as a placement director—as they go through their job search. The names used are unrelated to the actual students. We will see what they did and why, where they slipped, and how they ultimately succeeded.

ETHICS

An area of increasing interest to both students and career professionals is ethics in the job search. I have been actively involved in the area of ethics for several years and have served on the national Principles for Professional Conduct Committee of the College Placement Council. My article on "Ethics in Our Profession" won me the 1990 Hardwick Award. It is simply not true that "All's fair in love, war, and job searches." Success without honesty is failure. You will find discussions of ethics in the job search appropriately placed throughout this book.

WHAT WILL YOU GET OUT OF THIS BOOK?

Susan and Lauren lived in the same sorority house. Lauren joined the Job Search Club described in Chapter 1. She spent the hours and energy necessary to examine the corporate world, a role for herself in it, and her Positive Characteristics. She wrote many drafts of her résumé and prepared diligently for each interview. When she graduated, Lauren went to work as a financial analyst for a major firm at a starting salary of $28,000 plus benefits.

"Sometimes, I went a little crazy trying to balance my job search, classes, and part-time job," Lauren admitted. "I missed a lot of TV shows and some good parties. Unfortunately, my academics suffered a little bit and I missed a few days at my job. But it was worth it because now I'm starting my career with a good job that has good career prospects in a good company. Achieving that was one of my important goals in going to college."

Susan did not joint our Job Search Club. She was too busy to follow the advice in this book. Susan never missed a class, an hour of work, a party, or a TV show. She didn't have very much interview anxiety, because her résumé didn't win Susan many interviews. Unfortunately, Susan graduated without a job. Four months after graduation, she took a dead-end survival job with low pay and no benefits.

Do you really have to follow my advice here? The choice is yours.

What will this book do for you? It will help you work hard, smart, and ethically, in order to succeed in your job search. In short, it will help you become well-employed.

RICHARD FEIN

Amherst, Massachusetts
July 1992

Acknowledgments

As an author, I am indebted to many people. My thanks to Tad Tuleja, who patiently guided me during my early efforts at book writing. Dr. Robert Greenberg of the University of Tennessee and Dr. Richard White of Rutgers University, fellow placement directors, reviewed my manuscript. I deeply appreciate their help. Robert Pike of Procter & Gamble and Vaughn Rist of Spalding Sports Worldwide, corporate human resource professionals, read my manuscript and gave me helpful advice. My thanks also to Dr. Ron Fredrickson at the University of Massachusetts, whose insights as an educator were very useful.

To my wife, Rhonda, who knows what I'm like when I'm writing and still loves me, my deepest gratitude.

R.F.

Contents

FIRST JOB

PART ONE

Finding Out

CHAPTER ONE

Getting Ready for the Race

Think back 16 years or so, to about the time you entered kindergarten. Since then, you've grown through childhood and adolescence to adulthood. Throughout all the changes in those years, one thing has probably remained constant: You've been in school—you've been a student.

After 16 years of schooling, you're probably glad to be graduating from college and entering the "real world." But have you changed your thinking to reflect your new reality? You're about to go through another transition, from college student to corporate professional. It's time to start thinking about yourself as a corporate professional rather than "just a student." Begin to *see* yourself as a corporate professional and you'll be more likely to carry out an intelligent job search that will actually *make* you one.

THE JOB SEARCH CLUB

A good way for students to succeed in a job search is to share their experiences and ideas with other students. Working with groups of students is time-efficient, but a greater advantage is that students benefit from each other's comments, questions, and experiences.

> This book presents the Job Search Club members simply to *illustrate* how to conduct your own job search. By following the advice given here, you can proceed with your own search as an individual, or with a group of friends.

To help you with your job search, I will take you through the experiences of seven members of a Job Search Club. As I noted earlier, these are *composite* characters, not individual students with whom I have worked over

A Level Playing Field?

Our Job Search Club contains a mixture of liberal arts students and business majors. This mixture raises two questions:

Does a choice of major play a big role in a student's getting a job?

Are liberal arts majors on a level playing field with business students?

A student's choice of major often does play a role, but not the leading role, in a job search. For example, Alice, an accounting major, has an advantage in a search for a position in accounting or finance, because of her technical training. However, a college graduate's major isn't the only thing an employer looks for. Leadership, analytical ability, and communication, among other skills, are also important. Alice isn't guaranteed a job offer in the public accounting field; a liberal arts major like Robert may get one instead.

As for competing on a level playing field, the answers are "No" *and* "Yes."

"*No,*" in part, because business majors do have more course work in subjects directly applicable to running a business enterprise. But *the main difference is attitude.* Business students, by their very choice of major, tend to have a positive attitude about a business career. Many liberal arts students have been told, by parents, peers, or professors, that business education is really "trade school" and not a true education at all. They may also have been told that business is corrupt, immoral, and dominated by plutocrats. This condescending and hostile (and *inaccurate*) view of business strongly disadvantages liberal arts majors in seeking a job in corporate America. Skills can be taught more easily than attitudes can be changed.

Liberal arts students *can* compete on a level playing field if they can demonstrate a positive attitude toward business, a sense of reality about business life, and a familiarity with the issues that today's businesspeople must confront.

By doing their work as members of our Job Search Club, our liberal arts majors (David, Gabrielle, and Robert) will be able to compete successfully on any corporate job search playing field.

the years. These students' experiences are good learning tools for you. We will follow our seven club members from the awkward beginning of their job searches to their successful conclusions.

Details will unfold during their job search process. For now, let's identify the seven active members in this chapter of the club as college seniors at a fine (but fictional) institution we will call Emeritus College in Nebraska. Here are a few facts about them:

Alice: An accounting major who came to Emeritus from Illinois; has done well academically and has been active in extracurricular affairs.

Bill: Served in the Army for three years before coming to college; a marketing major.

David: A highly articulate student of history who views businesspeople as venal and selfish; concerned that working for a corporation may compromise his principles. (By coincidence, his work experience is much like Lauren's.)

Gabrielle: A political science major who doesn't have a clue yet about her career plans; joining the Job Search Club as a first major step forward.

Hector: Eats and breathes finance; pursuing a goal of becoming the chief financial officer (CFO) of a major company someday.

Lauren: A bright finance major best known among her peers for being socially astute; a mature young woman with no sense of direction about her career.

Robert: An anthropology major who is beginning to think about a career in public accounting or finance; wonders whether a liberal arts major can make it in those fields.

THE EVENT

Most people in college eventually realize that they're not going to be students forever—they *will* be looking for a job someday. The good news is that some students will start their job search preparation as juniors, or even sophomores, through attending job fairs, gaining work experience, or assuming leadership positions on campus. The bad news is that too many students won't begin thinking about a career until after graduation. Generally speaking, those who start preparing for a career before senior year are ahead of the game; those who wait until graduation are behind the eight ball. Students who seriously begin their search at the beginning of senior year are typical players in the job search game. With preparation and hard work, those who are in the game (or ahead of it) can emerge as winners.

What gets students to start a job search? Career specialists often refer to *The Event*—something that jump-starts a person into action. For college students, The Event can be: choosing a major, experiencing a meaningful summer job, being prompted by a friend or family member, hearing a guest speaker in a classroom, beginning some on-campus interviewing, or facing the bittersweet realization that graduation is inevitable.

Whatever serves as The Event in your life, the sooner it jump-starts your job search motor, the better off you'll be. You need time to draft and redraft your résumé to identify prospective employers and to prepare for your interviews. Getting a good job is the result of a *cumulative process.* You won't get a good job by last-minute cramming.

WHAT YOU NEED TO KNOW ABOUT YOURSELF

A critical part of your job search is getting to know about yourself. Of special importance are your own Positive Characteristics, the qualities that would make you an asset to an employer. What are your Positive Characteristics? What skills and attributes have you demonstrated, achieved, and learned that would be helpful in a professional context?

There are several ways to identify your Positive Characteristics and their importance to an employer. The next section gives you a Short Self-Profile (SSP), to get you started.

A SHORT SELF-PROFILE

I am not opposed to utilizing the well-known self-assessment exercises available to students today. However, I don't emphasize them, for three reasons:

- If you want to take advantage of exercises like the Strong–Campbell Interest Inventory or Myers–Briggs Type Indicator, you should see your college counseling or placement office. There is no point in having this book duplicate those resources.
- I emphasize the value of learning about the corporate world, and your possible place in it, by meeting with practitioners. For your transition from college to corporation, it's important to rely less on familiar academic methods, like tests, and more on beneficial business methods, like direct meetings.
- One purpose of this book is to help you get many job interviews. The interview process itself gives you an opportunity to assess yourself in the context of specific jobs or companies.

I designed the Short Self-Profile (SSP), shown in Figure 1.1, and I use it with students to achieve two major goals:

- Identify their Positive Characteristics;
- Give support, through examples, to Positive Characteristics students want to identify for themselves and convey to others.

Figure 1.1   A short self-profile.

	POSITIVE CHARACTERISTICS	
	Demonstrated, Achieved, Learned	*How, When, Where*

Demonstrated

	Here are two skills and two personal attributes that I demonstrated in the past four years.	Here is an example of how I used each skill or attribute and a reason why the skill or attribute would be important to an employer.
Alice	1. Leadership is an important skill. It's ability to inspire and direct. 2.	1. Informal leader of department at Good Buy Department Store. Skill of leadership is a key to utilizing personnel well, often a prerequisite for promotion. 2.
Bill	1. Self-starting. I don't need to be prodded to get moving on a project. 2.	1. Started my term papers and presentations at earliest possible date; also tracked down errant orders at Good Buy. Good for employer because he or she won't need to be looking over my shoulder. 2.
Gabrielle	1. Patience. I can take the time to make sure the job is done well, and I'm patient with others. 2.	1. Last year, worked with sorority pledges to get them actively involved in house; others had suggested I give up on them. Helpful to employer because I do a job right the first time; I develop staff and don't just demand results from them. 2.
Hector	1. My ability to analyze problems; I break a problem into its components. 2.	1. Analyzed reasons for receivables backlog at Toolco. Analyzing sources of problems is first step to solutions, and solving problems is essential to most professions. 2.

Figure 1.1 Continued.

	POSITIVE CHARACTERISTICS	
	Demonstrated, Achieved, Learned	*How, When, Where*
	Achieved	
	I achieved some things that an employer should know about. I include here at least one job-related example, one that shows personal or academic growth, and one from my civic or extracurricular involvement.	The context of each achievement, what it shows about me as a person and what qualities were needed to accomplish it are described here.
Alice	1. Ability to communicate with people from different ethnic backgrounds and scattered sections of the United States. 2. 3.	1. Residence hall advisor. Shows openness and respect for differences among people. Required patience and willingness to try something new. 2. 3.
Hector	1. Confidence in ability to do quantitative work. 2. 3.	1. In accounting and finance core courses. Shows I don't give up easily. Required ability to take my lumps when trying to get on top of difficult material. 2. 3.
Lauren	1. Proficiency in handling accounts payable paperwork. 2. 3.	1. Last summer, at Smallco. Shows ability to get a handle on new situations quickly. Required determination because I hate details and paperwork. 2. 3.
Robert	1. Savings of $50/month, through better ways to pay bills and save electricity. 2.	1. At Fruit Store. Shows I'm always thinking and I analyze situations well. Required gathering data, comparing actual and projected costs, presenting ideas to store owner.

Figure 1.1 Continued.

POSITIVE CHARACTERISTICS	
Demonstrated, Achieved, Learned	*How, When, Where*

Achieved

3.	2.
	3.

Learned

	Here are some things I have learned in and apart from school in the past four years.	*Here is how I learned these things about myself or these skills, and why learning them is important.*
Bill	How to manage time well.	Balanced academics, a part-time job, and extracurricular activities: Time is a valuable resource in business.
David	I don't have to be "the best" to be "good" at something; I can be accepted for who I am.	Made friends with classmates who were better at subjects than I am; found I was well-liked on jobs, even though I was just learning the ropes: I'm a lot happier when I don't think I have to be the best.
Gabrielle	How to slog my way through something I didn't like.	Didn't like my summer job, but stayed with it: Not everything in life is enjoyable.
Lauren	How to communicate ideas effectively; how to be brief or silent, when necessary.	Enlisted professor's help in political science course; participated actively at sorority meetings: Ideas, problems, and instructions need to be clearly communicated.

EXAMPLES*

My Leadership

Alice	In charge of group research and presentation for Management 301. Classmates participated and felt it was a success.
Hector	Organized "Casa Latina" cultural programs and got most members involved in some activity.
Lauren	Convinced co-workers at Good Buy to finish setting up displays before Chairman's visit to our floor. The group had to miss lunch to do it.

Figure 1.1 Continued.

My Problem Solving

David	Solved problem of ethnic tension in residence hall, in two ways. First, organized a Multiethnic Foods Festival ("Pig-out with a Pal"). Then, had open meeting on floor to discuss both good things and problems in the residence hall.
Gabrielle	Solved problems (returns of wrong-size or damaged goods; billing problems) for customers at Consumer Heaven department store. Learned to listen, be patient, and think quickly. (All the while, I hated that job.)
Robert	Solved problem of wasted time in the computer lab. Started policy of appointments for computer stations during high-use hours.

My Communication Skills

Alice	Professors have noted on my term papers, that I express myself clearly.
Bill	My best examples are from the residence hall, but, to identify at least one different environment, my class presentations generally get As or better grades than my test scores.
Hector	On summer job, wrote short memos requesting information. Learned how to be to-the-point without being abrupt. Memos must have been clear because I got what I asked for.

Difficult Situations and How I Resolved Them

David	When I visited Metropolis, I got lost looking for my friend's house. I was approached by two muggers who demanded my wallet and my suitcase. I gave them my wallet but convinced them there was nothing valuable in the suitcase.
Gabrielle	When I was Membership Chair of the Management Club, there were some serious personality conflicts. Some people didn't want to join because "those people" were in the club. I persuaded the President to establish some additional committees to attract the potential new members.
Lauren	Last summer, I discovered a major mistake in a report that had already been handed in to my manager. If I had pointed out the error, a permanent staff member, who was already on thin ice, would have been in trouble. If I hadn't corrected the error, my boss would have had bad information. Instead of showing my boss the error myself, I showed it to Tom, the person who made it. In that way, he was able to "catch" his own mistake. Tom was grateful.

Figure 1.1 Continued.

My Organizing Ability

Alice   I had a humongous load of data to go through for my part-time job. I organized my work load by outlining what I needed and listing the steps I needed to take. Then I organized the data by making a chart that showed where I could find what information.

David   Last summer, I organized an employees' softball team. There was some competition among departments, so it wasn't easy to get people to play together. I convinced folks we might cooperate more at work if we competed on the playing field.

Hector   This is a really hard semester for me. I organized my two part-time jobs to let me take the courses I wanted.

My Ability to Persuade

Bill   Persuaded the boss at my summer job to let me work on a PC, to handle some records. Had to overcome his objection that I had no PC experience.

Gabrielle Persuaded a professor to give us an option between a term paper and a final exam. Based my pitch on "diversity in education."

Lauren   Persuaded my sorority sisters to expand our membership. We needed to increase revenues, but they were afraid of overcrowding the house.

---

*The ideal target is three examples in each category, but the quality and relevance of the examples are more important than their number.

The first part of the SSP asks you to identify what you have demonstrated, achieved, or learned during the past four years. (The four-year time frame corresponds more or less with the years of your college experience.) There is no need to limit yourself to *classroom* experience. At least half of what you cite should reflect your experiences on jobs, in extracurricular activities, or in travel.

The second part of the SSP asks you to give *specific examples,* from your experiences, for six Positive Characteristics that are highly valued by employers. In your first try, you may find it difficult to cite as many Positive Characteristics or examples as the SSP requests. That's all right; the important thing is to get started. Write at least one Positive Characteristic or example for each item requested. You can return to the SSP periodically over the next few months until you complete it.

By working on the SSP, the members of the Job Search Club gained:

- Identification of some Positive Characteristics that they could utilize in their résumé and/or interviews.
- Credibility for their Positive Characteristics by giving them context and supporting examples.

When the Job Search Club members met to discuss their SSPs, they reached the following general conclusions:

- Examples are important because they lend credibility to what you say and they help you to clarify *for yourself* what you really mean.
- An example with a significant context supports and strengthens statements of Positive Characteristics. A relationship with co-workers probably provides a more significant context than a relationship with roommates.
- No one expects a college student to set the world on fire. To show time-management skill, you can show that you successfully balance conflicting demands in your *current* life (academics, job, extracurricular activities). A prospective employer then has a strong basis for believing that you will balance conflicting demands on your time in your future business life.
- It's best to develop examples from different life experiences—jobs, travel, and so on.

In this chapter, we met the Job Search Club members and saw how they began to identify their Positive Characteristics. The next chapter matches those characteristics to the demands of the business world.

CHAPTER TWO

Qualifications for Business Jobs

In this chapter, we shall see how the Job Search Club (JSC) examined characteristics that are important to typical business jobs. The Club had two main objectives:

- To identify important characteristics for jobs that were of interest to at least one JSC member;
- To learn how to research important characteristics for *any* job.

This book focuses on the importance of these characteristics to résumé writing and interviewing. In general, this information could also be important for determining what careers to pursue.

To accomplish our two goals, I asked the Club members to write on a file card the title of any business job that was of interest to them. All the file cards were put into a hat. Each member pulled out one card and was assigned to research that business job, whether or not it was of personal interest. At the end of the exercise, all the research was to be placed in a binder for the rest of the Club's benefit.

This is the way our job research lottery turned out:

Club Member	Job to Research
Alice	Retail management
Bill	Financial analyst
David	Sales representative
Gabrielle	Accountant
Hector	Market researcher
Lauren	Actuary
Robert	Personnel manager

The *process* for researching most business jobs would be the same for each Club member. Only the details would change.

RESEARCH SOURCES

I asked the JSC members what sources they might want to use in their research. This is a summary of what they suggested:

- SIGI PLUS® Computerized Career-Planning Software Program*
- Recruiting literature
- Career literature
- Professional associations
- Professionals in the field

Let's take a brief look at each of these sources.

SIGI PLUS

SIGI (System of Interactive Guidance and Information) PLUS is a computerized career-planning program produced by the Educational Testing Service of Princeton, New Jersey. It is available in over 1,000 colleges across the United States and in many noncollege libraries.

The SIGI PLUS program is an extremely useful tool because it lets the individual interact with it at his or her own pace. SIGI PLUS has eight core sections plus an introduction, but, for the purpose of this exercise, the JSC members used primarily the section called "Skills." This section helps users to learn what skills are needed in an occupation and to assess whether they have those skills. Thus, among other benefits, "Skills" gives users a list of the skills and attributes (similar to what we call Positive Characteristics) that are important in each of over 200 occupations.

One of the many useful features of the SIGI PLUS program is that it provides examples of the attributes it identifies. For example, if the skill is Analyzing, SIGI PLUS will give examples of how analyzing would be useful in the profession being researched. SIGI PLUS also gives examples of how the skill of analyzing might be used in various other aspects of life.

Although it was not a formal part of this exercise, the SIGI PLUS program was used by the JSC members to construct a generic job description for each profession they researched. They did this by compiling the SIGI PLUS descriptions of how each desirable skill for a given profession might be used.

* SIGI PLUS and the SIGI PLUS logo are registered trademarks of Educational Testing Service. The SIGI PLUS system is the proprietary software program of Educational Testing Service, Princeton, NJ 08541, and is available only under license from ETS.

For the purpose of this exercise, "Skills" was the most important section in SIGI PLUS. However, in general, I recommend spending time with all eight core sections.

Recruiting Literature

Many firms, particularly those that recruit actively among forthcoming college graduates, produce literature designed to attract student interest. "Why You'll Be Happy Working for Us" brochures are, in some measure, advertisements and should be taken with a grain of salt. However, they often contain information about specific skills that are useful to a particular profession or firm. The rest of the information in these brochures can be very handy in preparing for interviews.

Career Literature

Knowledgeable authors have written about many careers, both business and nonbusiness. We will review some of the literature the JSC members used for this exercise.

Professional Associations

The publications of professional organizations can be good sources for information about an occupation: the needed skills, desirable training, and job outlook. A very complete guide to these groups is Gale's *Encyclopedia of Organizations*. JSC members found that the quality of literature about professions varies from organization to organization.

Professionals in the Field

Practicing professionals are a *terrific* source. We dedicated a special meeting of the JSC to this subject. Chapter 3 examines "the pros" as a source of in-depth information.

HECTOR'S EXPLORATION OF MARKET RESEARCH

Hector's research assignment was a career in market research. His personal interest was in finance, so Hector wasn't thrilled with his topic. "Some things we do in life aren't fun," Hector thought, "but they're still worth doing."

Hector's first stop was at the SIGI PLUS computer. Choosing the "Skills" section from the SIGI PLUS menu, Hector typed in "165," the SIGI PLUS code for market research analyst. The SIGI PLUS program gave Hector this summary of skills:

Advising
Supervising, directing
Making presentations
Writing
Keeping records, cataloging
Gathering information, conducting research
Analyzing, interpreting, evaluating
Making diagrams
Analyzing numerical data
Working with computer

Hector was curious about the role of "analyzing, interpreting, evaluating" in market research. When the skill was keyed for more details, SIGI PLUS gave Hector a partial answer by showing this information on his screen:

ANALYZING, INTERPRETING, EVALUATING

In this occupation you might use this skill for tasks like these: Evaluate effectiveness of company's advertising campaign; conduct survey designed to find reasons behind recent plunge of product's sales figures; spot trends in consumer buying habits.

Hector realized that the same skills of analyzing, interpreting, and evaluating that he would need in finance had applications in market research as well. "Similar skills; different context and application," Hector noted.

Hector was right. Later, he used the SIGI PLUS program to do some research into financial analysis. Under "analyzing, interpreting, evaluating," Hector found this information: "Study set of new tax laws to determine whether company is eligible for tax breaks; check efficiency of company's inventory control system; study impact of proposed merger on company's standing in financial markets."

When Lauren researched the actuary profession through SIGI PLUS, she found these uses for "analyzing" in that profession: "Determine which factors influence frequency of car accidents among young adults; assess impact of work force layoffs in workers' contribution to union health insurance plan."

Our JSC members learned an important lesson: Many of the same skills are used in a number of professions, although with different applications.

Hector also noticed that a market research analyst would need some "soft" skills (advising, supervising) and communication skills. He made a mental note to research the relative balance between interpersonal and analytical skills in this profession.

> • The SIGI PLUS program is self-guided and easy to use. We were able to look at what Hector found without going through a step-by-step analysis of which buttons to push to access SIGI information.
> • If your college or library doesn't have SIGI PLUS, it may utilize another helpful computerized career-planning program or other career-planning tools.

When Hector found the *Occupational Outlook Handbook* (OOH) on a list of career resources, he decided to examine it in the reference section of our library.

The first thing Hector discovered was that economists and market research analysts were discussed in the same few pages of the OOH. "I'll bet those two jobs have a lot in common," Hector thought.

Hector read through the text. The first sentence told him concisely that "Market research analysts are concerned with the design, promotion, price, and distribution of a product or service." "How do they do that?" Hector said to himself. By carefully reading the text, Hector identified some Positive Characteristics similar to those he had learned from the SIGI PLUS program—collect data, code, evaluate, recommend (SIGI PLUS said "advising"), tabulate (SIGI PLUS said "analyzing numerical data")—and an additional skill: determining the advisability of potential courses of action.

Hector began to see the market research analyst as a major contributor to strategy, not just a numbers cruncher.

> The OOH is not the only career literature to utilize, but it is thorough and concise—two important virtues to consider when you are doing research.

Hector didn't end his research with the OOH. He found *Getting into Advertising: A Career Guide* by David Laskin to be interesting. "I know that it can be helpful to look into related fields," Hector reasoned, "and advertising must rely a lot on market research." Hector was right. *Getting into Advertising* contained a whole chapter on market research. Two sentences especially struck Hector:

Yes, you must know about statistics, but you bring to it an element of humanity. If we are really and truly to respect the consumer, we have to have a knowledge of what people are all about and why they are motivated to do certain things.

These sentences gave Hector a better understanding of what the SIGI PLUS program said about the need to "find reasons" and "spot trends in consumer buying habits." "There is a human element, not just numbers," Hector reminded himself. The chapter went on to describe how the market researcher operates in an advertising agency. This piece of research took less than 30 minutes and yielded two key sentences that were helpful to Hector's JSC research.

There were three lessons in Hector's effort:

1. Sometimes a few lines that put a subject in a better perspective can be as valuable as several chapters of facts and figures.
2. It often pays to think broadly about the resources that might be helpful to you.
3. Books about careers will often tell a good deal more about a particular profession, career paths, and industry projections than about Positive Characteristics. Even though that information is not part of a JSC assignment, it is useful in deciding about careers and preparing for interviews.

Hector also read some recruiting literature from market research firms. Let's see what Hector learned from a firm I'll call Smirk Marketing Services. The Smirk brochure identified four functional areas related to market research: client services, project management, consulting, and analysis field production management. Hector noted that client services and consulting required a graduate degree, so he quickly passed over them. In the other two areas, Hector noted several skills that the SIGI PLUS program had identified, sometimes in slightly different terms. Among them were supervising and strong verbal and written communication.

He also found some additional Positive Characteristics—decisiveness, assertiveness, and time management.

In the half-hour it took Hector to read the brochure, he gained an employer's insight into some skills (Positive Characteristics) the SIGI PLUS program had noted. Hector also listed some personality traits he hadn't previously identified. His efforts were certainly bearing fruit.

A REWARDING EFFORT

Hector had learned a good deal about the Positive Characteristics required to succeed in the career he had researched. His research had taken about

Table 2.1   Positive characteristics important to seven typical business jobs.

Accounting

Advising; supervising, directing, assessing; writing, preparing reports; gathering information, conducting research; analyzing, interpreting, evaluating; computing and applying formulas; analyzing numerical data; attention to detail; working with computers; communication (oral and written); concentration, patience; working with people; responsibility, integrity; self-starting, taking initiatives; teamwork.

Actuary

Analyzing; calculating; applying formulas; using computers; advising; presenting, explaining; evaluating; facility with market statistics; assembling data.

Financial Analyst

Coordinating work with others; supervising, directing, assessing; making presentations; analyzing, interpreting, evaluating; planning, making decisions; computing and applying formulas; analyzing numerical data; attention to detail; advising; working independently.

Market Research

Advising; supervising, directing; making presentations; writing; keeping records, cataloging; gathering information, research; making diagrams; time management; analyzing numerical data; decisiveness; assertiveness.

Personnel

Training, instructing; advising, counseling, interviewing; coordinating work with others; supervising, directing, assessing; making presentations; writing, preparing reports; analyzing, interpreting, evaluating; planning.

Retail Management

Time management; courtesy; patience; communication; training, instructing; persuading, negotiating, selling; keeping records, cataloging; planning, making decisions; developing budgets; analyzing numerical data.

Sales Representative

Presenting; managing personnel; writing responsive reports; analyzing data; having knowledge of product; persuading, negotiating, selling; competitive spirit; developing ideas; handling paperwork, keeping records; resilience; gathering information, conducting research.

Some of the Positive Characteristics Hector had found were associated with perhaps one but not all of the subfields of marketing research. Hector included all of them in his JSC report. Anyone using the report to construct a résumé would probably be referring to marketing research in a broad sense, not to a specific subfield. However, because interview preparation should be more specific, anyone interviewing for a particular job would read the sources Hector had cited (and others) to identify the Positive Characteristics most relevant to that particular job or subfield.

two hours. The yield in understanding had certainly been worth the time Hector had invested.

The other six members of the Job Search Club also had fruitful research investments. Table 2.1 summarizes what the JSC found out about the importance of Positive Characteristics for employment in seven typical business jobs.

SAME BOAT, DIFFERENT OARS

The Job Search Club met to discuss what they had learned from researching the Characteristics that were important to the typical business jobs. This is a summary of the conclusions they reached:

- Most jobs utilized more skills, and played a bigger role in adding value to a firm's business, than the Club members had realized.
- Some skills (Positive Characteristics) seemed to be important to most of the jobs the JSC had researched. These included advising, analyzing, communicating, interpersonal skills, and time management.
- A few hours of research could provide a good basis for learning about the skills needed in various professions and how they would be applied.
- To go beyond the basics about professions that were available in books, we would need to meet with professionals in the field.

The JSC members had learned how to begin their research about the characteristics that are important to typical business jobs. In the next chapter, we will see how a JSC member took the next step: asking people who actually do the job what it's really like.

CHAPTER THREE

Asking the Pros: The Informational Interview

This chapter explains four aspects of learning about careers and about yourself:

1. The value of pencil-and-paper self-assessment exercises;
2. How to identify and approach professionals, to ask about their professional lives;
3. What you can ask at an informational interview;
4. How to make use of what you learn at an informational interview.

> At an informational interview, you gather information about a profession or firm by asking a practitioner. The focus is on finding out what the profession actually involves, what it takes to succeed in the field, and what financial and personal rewards are available. You are inquiring about a profession, not asking for a job.
>
> A job interview, by contrast, is your chance to persuade a firm to hire you. It is much more of a selling experience than a learning experience.

SELF-ASSESSMENT: PERSONS INSTEAD OF PAPER

Unlike most job search guides, this book does not concentrate on paper-and-pencil self-assessment exercises, for three reasons:

- Most college students won't sit down to do them anyway.
- For those who are interested in that type of self-assessment, exercises are available in many books and counseling help is available at most colleges.

- This book is designed to give you *new approaches that work,* not to regurgitate available material. I will show you how to achieve the basic goals of self-assessment in a better way.

I am *not* saying that well-known exercises like the Strong–Campbell Interest Inventory or the Myers–Briggs Type Indicator are useless. To the contrary, they can be helpful and I encourage you to explore these exercises with a trained career guidance counselor. However, these exercises are neither absolutely necessary nor sufficient, as I will show you in this chapter. Those students who pursue paper-and-pencil self-assessment exercises will benefit more by looking up from their desks and finding out about professions from practicing professionals.

To move from the academic world to the corporate world, you need to become more familiar with corporate approaches and to rely less on the ways you're used to, like testing. If paper-and-pencil testing were a necessary or sufficient approach to hiring, firms would use them. Most firms don't.

Find out about the world of professional employment and what's in it for you by asking the pros—people who are experienced in the field you want to enter. What is it like to work in the treasury division of a corporation? Ask someone who is doing the job. Is the lucrative potential of a sales career worth the stress and uncertainty? Ask a sales professional. What does "work with people" mean? Ask someone who spends most of a professional career doing that. Is advertising really glamorous? Ask advertising professionals. Their answers may surprise you.

IDENTIFYING GOOD CONTACTS

David, a marketing major, came to see me early in his senior year. "I'm going to graduate in May," he said. "I enjoy my course work, but I don't know what I want to do for a living." I told David that his indecision was not unusual and asked him what kind of careers he had been considering. He told me he was thinking about sales, retail management, and market research.

"David, I think it's fine to be interested in three career paths at this point. I only get worried when people have *no* interests or a hundred interests. Let's think about our next step. What do you think it's like to be a salesperson, for example?"

David shrugged and said, "I'm not sure. I guess you have to talk a lot and be persuasive." David was only half right, but for the moment, I let it pass. "I think you're on to something here," I told David. "How do you think you could develop your understanding further?"

"I guess I could ask you," David said.

"You could ask," I replied, "but a placement director isn't your best source of information for the sales field. How about asking a sales professional?"

"That's interesting," said David, "but I don't know any."

"That's OK," I assured him. "Follow the Plowman's Principle."

DAVID'S OBJECTIVE

David thought about the situation. He wanted to learn more about a sales career, and speaking to sales professionals was one means to achieve

---

The Plowman's Principle:
Identify Your Objective, Then Plan How to Achieve It

How did the Plowman's Principle get its name? Frank, a farmer, had twin sons, Ralph and Dan, who were seniors in college. Although alike in most respects, Ralph and Dan approached their goal of owning a farm differently.

Dan thought about the situation this way: "I'd like to have a farm and harvest a great crop, but there are so many obstacles. My plow isn't sharp enough, my mule has never worn a harness, and the crows will probably eat my corn seed, anyway."

Ralph took a more productive perspective. "What's my goal?" he asked himself. "To own a farm," he answered. "What do I need to do? Let's see, first I'll buy a farm. Next, I'll buy a plow and a mule. Then, I'll plant my seeds. . . ."

Ralph knew he had obstacles, just as Dan did. But with his goal clearly in mind, Ralph identified ways to overcome the obstacles. Ralph said, "I'll buy a second-hand plow and make it as sharp as possible, even if it isn't the world's best. If my mule gives me trouble, I'll ask for help when I need to hitch her to the plow. I can put a scarecrow in the field to chase away birds."

The point is this: Many people torpedo their goals by identifying reasons why they can't achieve them. They destroy opportunities by getting things backward. The right way is this: First, identify your objective; second, identify what you have to do to achieve it. If you approach things this way, you will be able to move step-by-step to your goals, instead of getting discouraged before you really ever start.

Ralph can now be seen living his dream, plowing his field on a sunny day. Dan visits Ralph on weekends—if he isn't scheduled to work as a cashier in the local convenience store.

that goal. At first, David was concerned because he didn't know any professional salespeople. But, following the Plowman's Principle, we identified the goal (learning more about sales) and then figured out a means to achieve it. David and I decided to plan and execute an outreach program. We identified three categories of people who could be helpful:

- Warm calls—Family members, friends, and neighbors who would be glad to hear from him.
- Tepid calls—Friends of family members, families of friends, and other permutations of "warm calls."
- Cold calls—Complete strangers who could be helpful because they are practitioners in the profession David wanted to explore.

MAKING WARM CONNECTIONS

Getting started is often the hardest step for most people. Let's say that you, like David, don't have a friend, relative, or neighbor in the sales profession. I encouraged David to make a chart of his warm contacts. It was similar to Table 3.1, only bigger.

Of all the people on David's list of warm contacts, only David's cousin Jack was a professional salesperson. That was OK; better one than none. David was a little reluctant to call Jack because he didn't want to "mix business with family." I told David that rich people do it all the time; why shouldn't he? Besides, what are family and friends for? David called Jack, explained the purpose of his call, and arranged for an informational meeting the following Tuesday in Jack's office. Some people would have stopped seeking contacts until they had met with Jack. David was smart enough to keep right on pursuing possible contacts. He wanted to sustain his momentum and make good use of his time.

With only one of his relatives, friends, or neighbors a sales professional, David did seem to have a difficult row to hoe. Before his meeting with Jack, we took a closer look at his warm contacts chart together. His Aunt Millie was an accountant and his cousin Bob was a computer specialist.

At first glance, these relatives had been written off because they were not sales professionals. However, both of their employers probably had a sales force. I suggested that David contact his Aunt Millie, to ask her help in identifying a *consumer sales* professional in her firm, and his cousin Bob, to approach him about speaking with someone in *industrial sales*, because Bob worked for a firm producing tools for industry.

A social characteristic of American professional life is that people will be willing to speak to friends or relatives of a co-worker on an *informational* basis. Let's see how David arranged an informational meeting with Sheila, Aunt Millie's friend.

Table 3.1   Warm contacts.

	Relatives	

Immediate Family

		Uncles	
Father:	Public accountant	Sam:	IRS agent
Mother:	Lawyer	Arnold:	Weight lifter
Sister:	In college	*Cousins*	
Brother:	A pest (too young)	Louise:	Manager, Super Sale
Aunts		Jack:	Salesperson, Vacusweep Inc.
Millie:	Accountant, Cereal Inc.	Bob:	Computer specialist, Wrench Co.
Martha:	Aerobics instructor		

Friends

Bill:	Roommate, unemployed	Joyce:	Financial analyst, General Moods. (She said she wanted to be "still friends.")
George:	Had a summer position with Procter & Casino		

Neighbors

Harry:	Retired stock broker	Celia:	Homemaker
Edward:	Clergyman	Yvette:	Schoolteacher

NOT A BOWL OF CHERRIES

When David's Aunt Millie, an accountant at Cereal Inc., asked her lunch friend, Sheila, if she would be willing to speak to David about her experiences in sales, Sheila said yes. David knew Sheila was expecting to hear from him, so he skipped sending an introductory letter and called Sheila right away to set up a meeting.

David prepared carefully for the meeting:

- He read the Cereal Inc. annual report and studied basic facts about the firm and its products;
- He thought about how he would explain the purpose of his visit to Sheila: why he had gone to business school; what he wanted to find in his career; how Sheila could be helpful to him.

ADVICE FROM A PRO

David arrived at Cereal Inc. 15 minutes before his 10:00 A.M. appointment with Aunt Millie's friend, Sheila. After David met Sheila in her office, they exchanged pleasantries for a few moments. Then David led into the body of their discussion by:

David and I realized that we could expand the usefulness of his warm contacts chart with a little creativity. Deciding that David could productively go beyond contacting just Jack, Aunt Millie, and Bob, we looked at his chart (Table 3.1) again and made some notes:

Father: Public accountant. Perhaps he could ask one of his clients to speak to David.

Mother: Lawyer. Her specialty is consumer fraud; some potential there.

Sister: In college. Her boyfriend's father is a salesperson; doesn't hurt to ask.

Brother: Still hopeless.

Aunt Martha: Aerobics instructor. Maybe someone in her class is a salesperson.

Uncle Sam: Nice guy, but no clear connection.

Uncle Arnold: Maybe some of his friends who left athletics went into sales.

Louise: Manager at SuperSale. Salespeople from consumer products firms call on her all the time. They could be a *gold mine.*

Bill: Unemployed, but maybe one of his relatives is in sales.

George: He might help by speaking with the people he worked with on his co-op at Procter & Casino.

Joyce: General Moods has a sales force; maybe she can open a door.

Harry: Stock brokerage is a form of sales. *Call Harry!*

Edward: Clergymen want to be helpful. Maybe someone in the congregation is in sales. Salespeople join civic groups as well as churches. It pays to check this out.

Celia: She's a homemaker, but she's also involved in civic groups and she may attend a different church; double potential.

Yvette: As a schoolteacher, she knows lots of people in the community. No harm in asking.

David now has at least 13 more people to contact. Louise, George, Joyce, and Harry could be especially helpful.

Prepare or Fail

An informational meeting is almost like an interview. You must be prepared, in order to:

- Ask intelligent questions—a necessary step for getting useful answers;
- Influence the other person to give you the names of some of his or her professional friends and contacts, whom you can then add to your warm contacts chart. This is a very important way of expanding your connections.

You must understand that you are a business professional looking for a job, not "just a student." In business, you prepare before every meeting, and an interview, even one designed solely to gain information and insight, is like a business meeting. You can either prepare or fail. There are no shortcuts to success.

To prepare for his meeting with Sheila, David:

- Read some material on sales careers, borrowed from his college's career library;
- Researched Cereal Inc. by
  —reading Cereal's annual report;
  —finding recent published stories about Cereal Inc. and cereal in general in the business press;
  —visiting his local supermarket to see Cereal Inc. products on display.

David tried to speak with the supermarket manager about the manager's experiences with Cereal Inc. sales representatives. This was a great idea, but David was able to arrange a brief meeting only *after* his meeting with Sheila.

(For more details on researching firms, see Chapter 8 and learn what Alice and Hector did.)

- Thanking Sheila for scheduling their meeting;
- Acknowledging their time limit;
- Showing that he was prepared for a focused discussion;
- Asking for permission to take notes.

David said: "Sheila, I would like to thank you for putting some time aside for me this morning. I know your time is precious, so I'll keep our discussion within the 20-minute time frame we discussed when I called you. I've been exploring the possibility of going into a sales career and I'd really appreciate your advice. I have done some background research on Cereal Inc. and sales careers, but I also want to learn from a professional like you. It would help me if I could take notes. Do you mind?"

David then asked Sheila how she first got into sales and what she liked best about it. Did she enjoy scheduling her own sales calls rather than being in an office every day? How did Sheila persuade supermarket managers to position Cereal Inc. products where Sheila wanted them? (All of David's questions appear in the final section of this chapter.)

Sheila was impressed with David's questions, and their dialogue went past their 20-minute limit. David indicated to Sheila that their 20 minutes was almost up, and asked Sheila whether he could ask a few more questions. Sheila said, "Fine." She was energized by the quality of questions David was asking and by the fact that he obviously had come prepared. As the meeting progressed, David took the following notes on Sheila's comments, which reflected her perspective on sales:

- Sales can be lucrative.
- Selling to a customer is more listening than talking.
- Sales is a very competitive field.
- Rejection, frustration, and paperwork are all part of the job.
- Sheila didn't see anyone else from Cereal Inc. four workdays out of five.
- Sheila found selling to be an intellectual challenge.

As the meeting reached about half an hour, David again noted the time and suggested that perhaps they should wrap up. This time, Sheila agreed. David thanked Sheila for her time and assistance, and then asked for something more.

"Sheila, I want to thank you for your time and help. I've really learned a lot today.

"I'm going to continue my exploration of sales as a career. Could you give me the names of one or two of your sales colleagues whom I could also speak with."

Because David had come prepared with good questions, knew about Cereal Inc., and had some sense of what he might want in a career, Sheila readily agreed to give him the names of two other salespersons whom David could contact.

When David got home, he immediately did three things:

- Wrote Sheila a thank-you note;
- Called to thank his Aunt Millie;
- Reviewed his notes to see what he had learned.

WHAT DAVID LEARNED FROM HIS VISIT

There were two categories of new information for David to think about after he visited Sheila:

- What he had learned about sales, at least from Sheila's perspective;
- What he had learned about sales as a possible career.

Sheila had expressed satisfaction with her income; she had also described her job as intellectually challenging, in part because her field is so competitive and listening to the customer (not just the words but the intent) is so critical. Sheila didn't like the rejection, frustration, and paperwork. It didn't bother Sheila that on 80 percent of her workdays she saw no one else from her firm.

For Sheila, sales seemed to be a satisfying career, largely because the financial compensation and intellectual challenge offset the down sides of the field. David made a rough tabulation that included what his perspective would be if he had Sheila's job. (See Table 3.2.)

From his meeting with Sheila, David had learned some of the realities of sales. Actually, he had heard many of the facts before, in his sales management class, but hearing the experiences of a practitioner made the facts stand out sharply and come alive. For David, a more important outcome was being able to imagine how he would feel in Sheila's job. David noted these observations about himself:

- Money did not motivate him strongly.
- He was comfortable with competition in a sports context, but didn't like competition in other areas, such as academics.

Table 3.2   Perspectives on sales.

What Sheila Told David	Sheila's Perspective	David's Perspective
Lucrative	Very important	Nice, but not critical
Listening, not talking	A tool	A tool that could be learned
Competitive field	Sheila is a competitive person	Am I competitive (enough)?
Rejection, frustration, paperwork	Part of the game	A big drawback
Doesn't see others from Cereal Inc.	No big deal	Seems lonely
Intellectual challenge	A big plus	Very nice if it's a challenge

- Rejection, frustration, and paperwork would be a big grind for him.
- He felt a little lonely as he pictured himself out of an office four workdays out of five.
- He wasn't sure that what challenged Sheila intellectually would challenge him.

By reflecting on his reactions to specific facets of a sales career, David was learning a lot about himself.

TEPID CALLS

Encouraged by his success with Sheila, David expanded his chart of contacts by adding the names Sheila gave him and by developing the various permutations of his list of relatives, friends, and neighbors.

David asked his friends if they would:

- Give him the names of *their* relatives, friends, and neighbors who were sales professionals, whom David could contact;
- Let these people know that David, a friend of theirs, would be calling for *information*. Each friend who did this was making it more likely that David's request for information would be answered.

By expanding his outlook, David could now construct a chart that contained over two dozen warm and tepid contacts' names.

COLD CALLS

After meeting with four or five people from his warm and tepid contacts chart, David was ready to make cold calls—contacting people with whom he had no connection at all. He made a list of firms that were within

---

Cold calls are especially useful, for three reasons:

- They help you to become comfortable when speaking with strangers, a useful skill when you are actively looking for a job;
- You will be forced to travel away from your campus, which is a healthy way to see yourself as a professional who doesn't yet have a job, rather than "just a student";
- Although there is a limit to the number of your relatives, friends, and neighbors, there is no practical limit on the number of firms on which you could make cold calls.

commuting distance from his home or college. He called each company to get the name of the sales manager, or the person holding a similar title. He wrote each sales manager a letter, following the format shown in Figure 3.1.

Following up about a week later, David called each firm to which he had sent a letter. About one person in five was willing to speak with him on an informational basis.

Figure 3.1   Sample letter for arranging an informational meeting.

2468 Cornhusker Court
Lincoln, NE 68540
September 20, 1993

Mr. Paul Crane, Sales Manager
Hartfelt Industries
308 Farmington Avenue
Omaha, NE 68127

Dear Mr. Crane:

I am a senior at Emeritus College and have been investigating careers in sales. I plan on being in Omaha during the week of October 1 and will be talking with professionals like yourself who might provide guidance and advice about sales. I would appreciate fifteen minutes of your time, in order to learn more about sales, especially in an industrial environment.

For the past three years, I have earned most of my tuition by selling logo-shirts and painting fences. In my academic work, I have enjoyed the assignments and projects connected with sales and marketing.

I will call your office next week to see whether we can arrange a brief meeting. Any advice or direction you can offer will be greatly appreciated.

I assure you, Mr. Crane, that I am seeking information, not a job interview.

Sincerely,

David Peters

ARRANGING AN INFORMATIONAL MEETING

Before beginning his calls, David thought about what he was going to say. He knew that a smart, confident, polite presentation increases the probability that the other party will say "Yes." When David called Paul Crane at Hartfelt Industries, this is what he said.

David: Good morning, this is David Peters. Is Mr. Crane in?
Secretary: What is this in reference to, Mr. Peters?
David: I wrote to Mr. Crane last week, requesting a brief meeting purely for the purpose of learning more about the sales function.
Secretary: Mr. Crane is not available. May I take a message?
David: Yes; please tell Mr. Crane that David Peters called, as he had promised in his letter of September 20. I'll leave you my number, but in case Mr. Crane can't reach me, I'll call him again in a few days.

A few days later, David called again. This time, the secretary put the call through to Paul Crane.

David: Hello, Mr. Crane. This is David Peters. I hope you received my letter of September 20. As I indicated there, I would appreciate 15 to 20 minutes of your time to help me learn more about sales careers and the salesperson's function.
Crane: Are you sure we'll need only 15 minutes? Are you looking for a job?
David: I promise, 15 minutes. And, please, be assured: I'm not requesting a job interview. What I need is to get a clearer picture about sales, to help me make a sound career decision when I graduate from college next spring.
Crane: Fine. When do you want to come in?
David: Is early in the morning on Wednesday or Thursday good? Let's say, 8:30?
Crane: Let's make it at 8:00 A.M. on Wednesday, October 4.
David: Great. Wednesday, October 4, at 8:00 A.M. in your office. Thank you. I look forward to seeing you then.

Students should realize that every informational meeting is unique. David's list of questions provides only some *ideas* about questions you might want to ask.

Remember: Before you start asking your questions, you should explain your purpose, acknowledge the interviewee's kindness in spending time with you, and promise to be brief.

WHAT TO ASK AT AN INFORMATIONAL MEETING

David's questions, and their phrasing, are given here to get you started. Imitate their approach and their courtesy, but make them uniquely your own. Because this is an *informational meeting*, you should take notes.

1. I really appreciate your taking the time to speak with me this morning. Do you mind if I take some notes? My first question is this: Can you tell me how you started in this career? I'm especially interested in knowing what attracted you to the field. [The latter sentence is helpful because it enables the practitioner to address your interests more directly, and it doesn't burden the practitioner with a very broad, open-ended question.]
2. Please tell me some of the things you like best in your job and some things you would rather do without.
3. Can you describe your typical day or week? How do you spend your time on the job?
4. Are specific skills needed to succeed in this profession?
5. What kind of personal attributes tend to help a person do this job well?
6. Do you find this job challenging?
7. Can you tell me what you're feeling when work starts on Monday and when work ends on Friday?
8. How does your job affect your personal life?
9. Looking at your firm as a whole, how does your job add value to the company? What other people do you deal with, in the course of a week?
10. Were there any significant turning points or influences that affected your career?
11. If you could make a retroactive decision today that would change the way your career has developed, what would that decision be?
12. If I came to you and said, "I'm thinking about going into this field," what advice would you give me?
13. What factors outside your company tend to influence your professional life? The economy? Government regulations? Competing firms?
14. No one has a crystal ball, but how do you see the future of your firm, and others like it in the industry, over the next 5 or 10 years?
15. You've been extremely helpful to me. What you've told me has added to what I learned in class and through my research. [Give a few specific examples from your notes, if you can.] Could you suggest the name of someone you know who has a similar job, perhaps in another firm? I would like to continue learning about this profession from other professionals like yourself.

Hitches and Glitches

Record Keeping—Keep careful records of your informational interviews. You will want to spend some time, soon after your interview, evaluating what you have learned and organizing the names and addresses of new contacts.

Thank-you notes—These should be sent to each person you talked with at any length. A few lines can indicate your appreciation of the time they spent with you and of the value you derived from the interview.

By speaking with professionals who had different feelings about the same type of job, David realized that no one was an oracle speaking a Universal Truth or predicting David's future. Instead, David evaluated what each professional told him. He used the information to get a better perspective on sales as a career and on what a sales career would mean to him.

This chapter has given you a method to learn about professions, and about yourself in relation to them, by asking professionals. You now know how to identify contacts, how to approach them, what to ask, and what to do with the information you get.

Now you're ready for your next step: writing your résumé.

PART TWO

Résumé Writing

CHAPTER FOUR

The Tough First Lap

To win interviews, you must write a résumé that tells a prospective employer the time spent interviewing you will be worthwhile.

PROBABILITY, NOT A CRAP SHOOT

The hardest part of the job search process is getting invited to an interview. There are large numbers of applicants for most job openings. Once you are at the interview, you have survived the first cut and the odds are less weighted against you.

How do you get invited to an interview? Unless the prospective employer already knows you, your résumé will determine whether you get an invitation. View your résumé as a means to increase *the probability* of getting a job interview. Given its vital role, you should consider your time and effort spent on writing your résumé to be an investment rather than an expense.

The return on your investment will come in two ways:

1. You will be invited to more interviews, because good résumés earn interviews;
2. You will do better at each interview.

The preparation you put into writing your résumé, and the questions your résumé prompts your interviewer to ask, will increase your interview success rate.

When you are looking for a job, a résumé is usually a necessary part of your equipment. What is a résumé? It is a *brief* advertisement that conveys your message: "Interview me, because I am worth the investment of your time. Based on what I have shown about myself in the past, I am a good prospect for employment with your firm in the future."

Your résumé should be thought of as a way to present to an employer those Positive Characteristics that would make you a valuable employee. There are four key points to remember:

1. Your résumé is a presentation of *you,* not a series of job descriptions.
2. Your résumé must be *reader-friendly*—presented in a manner that is relevant, interesting, and clear to the reader.
3. Keep your résumé *brief;* it is not a life history.
4. A good résumé *increases the probability* of getting an interview, but there are no guarantees.

NOAH'S RÉSUMÉ

In Figures 4.1 and 4.2, two résumés are given for comparison. Take 60 seconds to read both of them, and assume that you must invite one (and only one) of the applicants to a job interview. Which applicant would you invite?

Ancient Dates

Noah lived about 6,000 years ago. Some people refer to that period of history as "B.C." and others as "B.C.E."

Whatever notation you would use, remember that the years with the *smaller* numbers are *closer* to our own period of history.

Over 5,000 undergraduate students have done the 60-second Noah exercise over the past 10 years. *Only two* students voted to invite Noah I to the interview. This response indicates two useful points:

- A better résumé increases the probability of your getting an interview, perhaps dramatically;
- Even an awful résumé will win an interview sometimes. With results like 4,998 to 2, you probably wouldn't want to bet your career on a poor résumé.

Neither of Noah's résumés is very good. The Noah I résumé is not directed to areas of the reader's interest and contains many irrelevancies. The Noah II résumé begins to address aspects of his experience that would interest an employer. Even so, Noah II could use considerable improvement.

Knowing that Noah could use a little help, let's imagine that Noah and I have worked through the *four steps of a winning résumé.* (By using the example of an ancient hero, we can see the *general principles* involved without being concerned yet about their application to résumés in the 1990s. In the next chapter, we will see how two members of the Job Search Club, with similar experience but different career goals, write *their* résumés.)

Fortunate Flaws

The Noah I résumé (p. 40) shouldn't be left to the archeologists. We can learn from its mistakes. Let's examine Noah I in some detail:

- *Useless information:*
  —The words "Name," "Address," and so on.
  —"Height," "Weight," and so on, are foolish; we don't hire by the pound.
  —References don't belong on a résumé. The reader probably doesn't know the people you mention, so their names mean nothing.
- *Message:* There is no Summary or Objective to convey Noah's message. What is the point of this résumé?
- *Not reader-friendly:* Relevant to a reader only if he or she cares about archeology. Should have conveyed and validated Positive Characteristics useful to a business career.
- *Awkward use of language:* What's the B.A.R. method? Avoid using acronyms or situation-specific terms, unless their meaning is immediately obvious to the reader. Examples of *acceptable* abbreviations would be USA or IBM.
- *Words that can be ambiguous or misconstrued:* Some students who read this exercise confused "castigated" with a severe physical mutilation of a male body.
- *Negative terminology:* Use positive terminology instead. Noah I refers to "one son who was a bum." Noah II presents the same situation well by stating it positively: "supervised rearing of three sons, with 67 percent success rate."
- *Graphics:* Noah I is hard to read. The Noah II résumé is more appealing to the eye. Key headings are in italics, and the spacing is better. Although *content* is your primary concern, graphics cannot be ignored. (Underlining can be substituted for italics.)

IDENTIFYING POSITIVE CHARACTERISTICS

My first suggestion to Noah was that he make a list of *Positive Characteristics* he would like any employer to know about him. Positive Characteristics are anything you have demonstrated, achieved, or learned that would help you to be an asset to your employer. Some characteristics are generally

Figure 4.1 Noah's résumé, first version.

Name:	Noah I	Height:	5'7"
Address:	Ararat Drive	Weight:	165 lbs.
City:	Ancient City, World 10001	Age:	106
Telephone:	(999) 666-5678	Health:	Excellent
		Married	

Experience

September 4283 B.C.E. to
June 4255 B.C.E.

Ark Builder
Among my responsibilities were: Built an ark of gopher wood, 300 cubits by 50 cubits by 30 cubits. Used the B.A.R. method to seal both inside and outside. Gathered different species of animals in pairs—two pairs if they were unclean animals and seven pairs if clean. Participated in sailing activities. Sent out both a raven and a dove. Disembarked after lengthy storm subsided. Castigated one son who was a bum.

January 4299 B.C.E. to
June 4284 B.C.E.

Self-employed
Built cabinets, ordered materials, performed all required bookkeeping functions.

Education

Attended regional elementary school—4 years.

References

Shem Noahson
93 Hilltop Road
Ancient City, World 10010

Yaphet Noahson
62 Valley Stream
Ancient City, World 10009

applicable to almost *all* professional-level jobs in business. Noah began to write the following list, based on information he had gathered from informational interviews, career fairs, and recruiting literature:

Organization
Leadership
Communication
Ability to solve problems
Hard-working
Meets or beats deadlines
Respected in community.

Figure 4.2   Noah's résumé, alternate version.

Noah II
Ararat Drive
Ancient City, World 10001
Office: (999) 888-1234
Home: (999) 666-5678

Career Objective: A challenging position in the design and administration of novel flood insurance policies.

Professional Experience:

4283–4255 B.C.E.   *Ark Builder*

Recognized impending world disaster before any contemporary. Built ark to save family and selected pairs from the animal kingdom. Navigated vessel through worst flood in recorded history. Reestablished human and nonhuman life on earth immediately after end of deluge. Supervised rearing of three sons, with 67 percent success rate.

Won "Righteous Man in His Generation" award.

4299–4284 B.C.E.   *Entrepreneur*

Established own carpentry business. Expanded enterprise from zero profit situation to highest income bracket of annual gross revenue.

Education:

Self-taught in religious philosophy, navigation, and animal husbandry. Awarded carpenter's tools while studying with my family.

Citizen of World

Willing to travel; willing to relocate.

References available on request.

I agreed that this was a good initial list that could be revised later if necessary. I also noted that this list could be useful in all of Noah's résumés, not just the one for flood insurance administration.

Next, I asked Noah to make a list of his Positive Characteristics that qualified him for the flood insurance business *in particular*. This is what Noah wrote, utilizing articles from a flood trade publication and an informational interview with Storm Jackson, an expert in the field:

Foresight
Experience with floods
Risk analysis.

I told Noah that these were interesting characteristics and, frequently, a job seeker's list of Positive Characteristics useful to employers *in general* was larger than the list of Positive Characteristics important for a particular kind of job.

By joining the two lists, Noah had identified the Positive Characteristics he wanted to convey and validate through his résumé.

WRITING EXAMPLES

Noah then began the second step of developing his résumé. He wrote *examples* for each of the characteristics he had listed. Noah took some of his examples straight from his Short Self-Profile (SSP; see Chapter 2). Others came to Noah's mind as he thought about this specific situation. Noah's inventory of examples is shown in Figure 4.3.

Why Examples Are Important

Your examples are important for you and for the reader of your résumé:

For you: They help you in making sure that you have a solid basis for any Positive Characteristic you want to convey.

For the reader: They help validate the claims of your résumé.

Noah and You

You may have noticed that Noah's primary strength seems to be work experience and that his education was rather limited. Noah will probably put the "Experience" section before "Education" on his résumé. For most American undergraduates today, the reverse order would be more effective. The section that will most impress the reader with Positive Characteristics should go first.

STATING AN OBJECTIVE

I convinced Noah that he would benefit from having a Summary (or Objective, if he preferred that term) at the beginning of his résumé, for the following reasons:

- A Summary would be a succinct and explicit method of conveying Noah's message to the reader;

Figure 4.3   Noah's inventory of examples.

Leadership:
Navigated ship through worst flood in human history.
Directed reestablishment of human life on earth.
Persuaded numerous pairs from the animal kingdom to board custom-made ark.
Convinced lions, lambs, and chimps to behave themselves on long voyage.

Organization:
Organized thousands of creatures to board ark in an orderly manner.
Organized construction project to assure that labor and material availability coincided.
Organized tools and material for easy access while establishing carpentry business.

Communications:
Advised humans that The End was near.
Convinced recalcitrant sons to assist in ark building.
Notified pairs from the animal kingdom to be ready on ark's departure date.

Ability to Solve Problems:
Solved logistic and staff problems inherent in ark building.
Solved lion/lamb problem by constructing separate quarters.
Solved carnivore diet problem by making veggie burgers that tasted like meat.
Solved problem of finding dry land by utilizing raven/dove dispatch method.

Meets or Beats Deadlines:
Completed ark before onset of flood.
Never left a customer waiting for finished goods in carpentry business.

Respected in Community:
"Righteous Man in His Generation" award.
Annual Raven/Dove Contest Chairman.

Hard-working:
Worked an average of 70 hours a week in carpentry business and 24 hours a day while navigating ark.

Foresight:
Anticipated and prepared for flood.

Experience with Floods:
Survived Flood and reestablished life on earth.

Risk Analysis:
Assessed risk of setting out to sea in an untested vessel.

- An Objective would serve as a *roadmap for Noah* as he wrote his résumé;
- An Objective would be a *roadmap for the reader* of Noah's résumé, by letting the employer know what profession interested Noah and what Positive Characteristics Noah would bring to the job;
- An Objective would lend *credibility* to Noah's application to prospective employers, by showing that Noah has a *focus* in his job search.

Message and Summary

Noah reviewed the list of Positive Characteristics he had just constructed, to determine the *message* he wanted to convey in his Summary. Noah kept in mind that his résumé should serve to show how his *past* is a good *predictor* of what he can contribute to an employer in the future. On that basis, this is the message Noah wanted to convey, presented in résumé language and format:

Summary: Proven skills in leadership, communication, and problem solving. Demonstrated ability to assess risk and respond appropriately. Professional experience with The Flood and reconstruction. Seeks to build a career in selling insurance, with a special interest in flood insurance. Interest developed as a result of leading role played in worst flood in recorded history.

There are two points to notice here. First, Noah has included in his Summary those Positive Characteristics he feels will most favorably impress the type of employer for whom the résumé is intended. Later, Noah could add or delete some phrases, if he felt it would be useful. Second, because Noah planned a separate résumé for every type of job he might pursue, I told Noah that he could be very focused about his career goal and supporting Positive Characteristics on any given résumé. The flip side would be that, if Noah planned a résumé with less specific focus, his summary would be less specific as well.

Now, using his Summary, Noah had a roadmap for writing his résumé. Noah went to work on the next step—writing a draft text.

WRITING A DRAFT TEXT

Noah pulled examples from his inventory and modified some of them. Then Noah used them to validate the message he had conveyed in his Summary. Let's look at Noah's initial draft, in Figure 4.4.

Noah and I assessed his first draft. It showed focus, highlighted the Positive Characteristics Noah wanted to communicate, and was logical. We knew, however, that it's always a good idea to take a closer look.

Figure 4.4 Noah's initial draft text.

Noah
Ararat Drive
Ancient City, World 10001
(999) 666-5678

Summary: Proven skills in leadership, communication, and problem solving.
Demonstrated ability to assess risk and respond appropriately.
Professional experience with The Flood and reconstruction. Seeks
to build a career in selling insurance, with a special interest in flood
insurance. Interest developed as a result of leading role played in
worst flood in recorded history.

Work   *Flood Beater*
Experience: Led rescue of human and animal life from the Great Flood. Directed
reestablishment of human life on earth. Assessed risk of destruction
based on heavenly insight and gathering rain clouds. Responded by
organizing thousands of creatures to board a custom-made ark in an
orderly manner.

Solved both logistic and staff problems while completing ark under
tight deadline. Communicated directly with ark passengers, thus
minimizing discord during forty rough days at sea. Learned how to
manage massive enterprise with minimal resources.

Carpenter
Built structures ranging from book shelves to family houses.
Designed ark decks and accommodations for selected clients.

Education: *School of Hard Knocks*
Bachelor of Biblical Administration
Major: Management

Honors: "Righteous Man in His Generation" awarded in recognition
of high moral character and trust of contemporaries.

Leadership   Chairman, Dove/Raven Contest; Vice President, Ararat 4-H
Activities: Society

When Noah and I looked at his Experience section, there were some
things we wanted to check. Had Noah validated the Positive Characteristics he had stated in his Summary? Because the Summary is a roadmap, the
résumé reader should be able to find in the rest of the résumé any Positive
Characteristic that the Summary mentions.

To make sure Noah's Experience section and Summary were correlated,
he made a two-column chart. First, Noah analyzed "Flood Beater":

Positive Characteristics in Summary	*Correlating Sentence(s) in "Flood Beater"*
Leadership	"Led Rescue . . ."
Communication	"Communicated directly . . ."
Problem Solving	"Solved both . . ." "Responded by organizing thousands . . ."
Risk Assessment	"Assessed risk of destruction . . ."
Appropriate Response	"Responded by organizing . . ."
Flood Survival and Reconstruction	"Communicated . . . during forty rough days at sea." "Led rescue . . . from the Great Flood." "Directed reestablishment . . ."

In this first draft, "Flood Beater" supplied at least one sentence to support each of the Positive Characteristics cited in Noah's Summary.

Next, we looked at Noah's work experience as a carpenter. We noticed that Noah's Carpenter section on his first draft résumé didn't validate any of his Positive Characteristics. We reexamined Noah's inventory of examples (Figure 4.3), to see whether something had been overlooked, and found these pairs:

Positive Characteristic	*Correlating Example for "Carpenter"*
Meets or Beats Deadlines	"Never left a customer waiting . . ."
Hard-working	"Worked an average of 70 hours a week . . ."

Noah was then able to make two improvements!

- Make the Carpenter section more useful;
- Add to the message the Summary conveyed.

The redrafted Carpenter section read as follows:

Carpenter:

Established own carpentry business; worked 70 hours a week. Met or beat all deadlines promised to customers for furnished goods.

To his draft Summary, Noah added ". . . hard worker; known for consistently meeting or beating deadlines . . . ."

At this point, Noah had drafted:

- A Summary that conveyed his message and was a roadmap for reading the Positive Characteristics he wanted to present. Noah made sure his roadmap was accurate by checking that the Positive Characteristics mentioned in his Summary were substantiated in the body of his résumé;
- An Experience section that validated the Positive Characteristics conveyed in his Summary.

Hitches and Glitches

- Noah's formal education was not extensive, so it is not discussed at length in his résumé.

    To make Noah's résumé look more like yours in format, we posthumously conferred on him a unique degree: Bachelor of Biblical Administration.
- We have not yet discussed other selling points (OSP) in regard to Noah's draft. Noah's OSP section has the headings "Honors" and "Leadership Activities." These OSP headings serve a purpose by covering a Positive Characteristic that could be very important in many professions, including flood insurance: being an honored member of the community.

    We will discuss other selling points more extensively in the next chapter.
- Your résumé is always in development; in that sense, it is always a draft. When you need to submit a résumé to a prospective employer, you use the best text available at that time. But your current draft can always be changed in some way.

    Unlike the Ten Commandments, your résumé is *never* carved in stone.

Noah had now prepared a usable draft résumé. Not bad for an Ancient.

In this chapter, we saw how Noah used four steps to write his draft résumé:

1. List your Positive Characteristics (general and particular);
2. Give examples to support your Positive Characteristics;
3. Write a Summary statement that conveys your message;
4. Prepare a draft résumé that validates your Summary.

In the next chapter, we will look at two Job Search Club members who share a nearly identical work history and see how and why they wrote two substantially different résumés.

CHAPTER FIVE

Same Work History but Different Résumés

Lauren and David, two members of our Job Search Club, were almost identical in their work history. These two seniors shared a good number of the same employment experiences:

- Residence hall (dormitory) counselor
- Retail store clerk
- Accounting department at Smallco
- T-shirt purveyor
- Waiter/Waitress.

In this chapter, we will see how Lauren and David presented themselves on their respective résumés. Even when two people have a similar history, they may write substantially different résumés.

Lauren and David were different in their academic choices and their goals:

- Lauren was a business major; David had majored in liberal arts;
- Lauren was considering a career as a financial analyst; David started senior year dubious about the legitimacy of the free enterprise system. Through his positive experiences in part-time jobs and our discussions in the Job Search Club, David decided to look for a job instead of a graduate school. David was thinking about sales as a way to make a living (see Chapter 3).

Both David and Lauren targeted four core résumé sections:

Summary or Objective;

Education;

Experience;

Other Selling Points.

The first step for each of them was to identify the Positive Characteristics they wanted their résumés to convey.

DAVID'S RÉSUMÉ

David's progress with his résumé benefited from having done a Short Self-Profile (see Figure 1.1) and from the work done by the Job Search Club members, including himself, when they held their informational interviews (see Chapter 3).

To see how David thought about his résumé, let's review his original list of Positive Characteristics, based on his research into sales as a profession:

Bright	Competitive
Innovative	Self-starter
Loves people	Team player
Works hard	Accepts rejection
Speaks well	Problem solver

I asked David to make an updated chart indicating the most important Positive Characteristics, his sources for knowing that these Positive Characteristics were important, and why he felt he could offer them. His chart is shown as Table 5.1.

From looking at his updated chart, David could see the Positive Characteristics he could offer that would be of interest to a sales professional. Some, but not necessarily all, of these characteristics should be part of David's message.

FOLLOWING IN NOAH'S FOOTSTEPS

David was now ready for the second step: identifying examples to support the Positive Characteristics he wanted to include in his message.

One of David's personal traits was thoroughness as a record keeper. For his examples, he could immediately draw on his notes from his SSP, his informational meetings, recruiting literature, and specialized books.

David enlisted all those sources to identify examples that would support the Positive Characteristics he wanted to convey in his message. An abbreviated version of David's list of examples appears in Table 5.2.

David has chosen examples from different parts of his life. This is a good idea. You are not a one-dimensional person. Why draw your examples from only one source?

Table 5.1 Positive characteristics important to the sales profession.

Positive Characteristic	Source of Identification	Personal Comments
Persuasiveness	Observation of salespeople	I have persuaded my peers in the Wild Eyed Radical Club to accept my point of view, a helpful skill.
Management of paperwork	Recruiting brochure	I do good research and keep accurate notes. I remember to follow up on incomplete research trials. Some people hate paperwork, but I can live with it.
Development of ideas	Sheila	I'm good at developing ideas for research papers; also, my ideas at
Intellectual challenge	Sheila	the Radical Club attracted attention and won converts.
Ability to Listen	Sheila	I've become a better listener since meeting with Sheila and partici-pating in the Job Search Club.
Competitiveness	Discussion with Uncle Jack at the family reunion	I'm probably more competitive than I used to think I was. I try to get the best grades in my classes, and I enjoyed beating my challengers to become president of the Radical Club.
Being a self-starter and team player	Recruiting literature	Some firms emphasize the ability to work on your own. Others focus on teamwork. I do my research on my own, but I'm a team player in the Radical Club.
Rejection	Sheila and Uncle Jack	I don't like rejection, but I learned to live with it when I was selling T-shirts last summer.

Table 5.2 Examples to support positive characteristics.

Persuasiveness

Persuaded peers in Wild Eyed Radical Club to accept my point of view. [David subsequently decided *not* to use this example. He realized that he wished to convey his *interest* in business, not his doubts about the legitimacy of free enterprise.]

Persuaded tourists to buy "politically correct" logo T-shirts.

Persuaded professor to allow me to write research paper instead of a final exam.

Figure 5.2 Continued.

Persuaded restaurant customers to order dessert and drinks with their meals, thus increasing their bills substantially.

Persuaded students in residence hall to join "Pig-out with a Pal" planning committee, even though they hated each other.

Management of Paperwork

Meticulous and thorough in keeping records to support my research papers.

Maintained records for T-shirt business; located missing logo shipment.

Development of Ideas

Developed ideas for investigating obscure points of information on Shay's Rebellion.

Developed ads for the tourist tabloids, to attract customers to T-shirt business.

Developed strategy to gain publicity for the Radical Club.

Developed "Pig-out" idea as means to reduce ethnic tension in the residence hall.

Intellectual Challenge

Love to investigate historical events and determine what was really behind them.

Found ways to improve lay-outs and displays at Good Buy department store. (I did it to save my sanity, but it worked.)

Studied history of the various ethnic groups in the residence hall so I could be a better counselor.

Ability to Listen

Listened to potential T-shirt customers, to determine what they wanted. (Made the sale a lot easier.)

Listened to restaurant customers, to help make menu recommendations.

Competitiveness

Tried to get highest grades in classes.

Beat competitors to become president of the Radical Club.

Purchased the most "in" logos, to attract customers away from other T-shirt hawkers.

Being a Self-Starter and Team Player

Don't need to be reminded to get research projects under way.

Initiated research into missing accounts receivable records at Smallco.

Proposed solutions to residence hall tensions on my own initiative.

Cooperated with cooks, busboys, and other waiters in the restaurant.

Worked with other residence hall counselors to resolve common problems.

Did joint research in sociology course on the impact of unemployment on family stability.

Rejection

Survived having ideas rejected by other residence hall counselors and the Dean of Students.

Rejected frequently by tourists who didn't buy my T-shirts. (But I kept on selling.)

A SUMMARY TO CONVEY YOUR MESSAGE

David had fulfilled the first two steps of a winning résumé: He had developed a list of his Positive Characteristics that would be meaningful to his intended audience, and he had supported each characteristic with examples. Now he was ready for the third step: articulating his message and writing a Summary that would convey it. From his list of Positive Characteristics and his examples, this is the message David developed:

> Innovative problem solver who develops and presents ideas well. Listens to others to build relationships. Self-starter who knows how to be a team player. Persuasive; able to overcome objections and accept rejections. Hard worker, competitive; thorough and accurate.

Based on his message and on what he had learned about himself through writing his examples, David wrote this initial draft Summary:

> Summary: Innovative problem solver, good listener. Persuasive presenter in both selling and social situations. Gained business sense through practical experience. Self-starter and team builder. Seeks to establish a career in sales leading to sales management. Interest in sales developed through practical sales experience and meetings with sales professionals.

From Message to Summary

Two things distinguish David's message and Summary: The Summary contains only the most important Positive Characteristics of the message, and the Summary adds a career goal and a motivation for wanting that career.

David wondered whether his Summary was too long. I told him that there is no firm rule about length. I suggested that David evaluate his summary on this basis:

Does it convey a message that would interest a potential employer?

If the Summary elicits and maintains interest, it is not too long.

If the Summary doesn't sustain the reader's interest, it is the *content*, not the length, that needs to be revised.

David evaluated his Summary and felt that it conveyed the most essential parts of his message and contained only material that would be of interest to a prospective employer. If space became a problem, one or two lines might have to be deleted from his Summary. Presumably, these would be lines with the least value for the reader.

Using his Summary as a roadmap, David proceeded with the fourth step, writing his draft résumé (Figure 5.1). He drew on the examples in Table 5.2, especially to write the Experience section of his résumé.

VALIDATING THE SUMMARY

David had worked hard on his initial draft, but had he validated his Summary? Before we showed it to the Job Search Club for comments and suggestions, we wanted to make sure that David's text had validated his Summary.

> "Text," as used here, refers to the Education, Experience, and Other Selling Points sections of a résumé.

David made a two-column chart (see Table 5.3) to see whether he had at least one example to support each of the Positive Characteristics conveyed in his Summary:

Looking at David's chart, we could see that:

- Every Positive Characteristic conveyed in his Summary was validated in the text of his résumé;
- He had used examples from five different work experiences. (It is a good idea to choose examples from different parts of your life.)

If your experience *doesn't* validate something from your Summary, should it take up space on your résumé at all? Here is how David handled his less relevant experience:

- Most of David's validating was done in his Experience section. His other selling points (OSP) (e.g., honors, computer skills, activities) did not add much and were placed at the end of his résumé.
- David's Education section basically said that David was smart. That's useful, but it doesn't need to be an explicit part of the Summary. David also "validated" the Positive Characteristic of hard work by indicating that he had "self-financed 60% of college tuition and living expenses," although he hadn't explicitly included that in his Summary either. That's OK. Sometimes, your text will support Positive Characteristics not included in your Summary.

David and I decided that it was time to discuss his draft with the JSC.

Figure 5.1   David's draft résumé.

David Peters

College Address   *Permanent Address*
2468 Cornhusker Court   1357 Loco Parentis Place
Lincoln, NE 68540   Madison, WI 53722
(402) 975-1357   (608) 531-2468

Summary: Innovative problem solver, good listener. Persuasive presenter in both selling and social situations. Gained business sense through practical experience. Self-starter and team builder. Seeks to establish a career in sales leading to sales management. Interest in sales developed through practical sales experience and meetings with sales professionals.

Education: Bachelor of Arts
Emeritus College (Lincoln, NE), May, 1993
Major: History   Minor: Sociology
GPA Major: 3.8   GPA Overall: 3.7
Self-financed 60% of college tuition and living expenses.

Research Papers: "Death of a Salesman—Will Willie Loman Ride Again?"
"The Salesman in American History"

Experience:

Academic Semesters:

The Slim Gourmet, Lincoln, NE. Waiter.

Persuaded customers to order drinks and dessert, thus increasing revenue for the restaurant. Trained new waiters in customer relations techniques. Worked 20 to 30 hours per week to pay college expenses. (Fall 1992–Present)

Residence Hall Counselor, Emeritus College, Lincoln, NE.

Established multiethnic food festival ("Pig-out with a Pal"), which alleviated intergroup tensions among residents. Listened to student problems ranging from loud stereos to serious depression. On call 24 hours a day. (Fall 1991–Spring 1992)

Summers:

Smallco, Omaha, NE. Accounts Receivable Clerk.

Initiated research into missing accounts receivable records; resulted in collection of $10,000 in overaged receivables. Learned how various functions must work together for business to be profitable. (1992)

Good Buy Department Store, Madison, WI. Section Supervisor.

Developed new lay-outs and merchandise displays, which increased customer activity by 20%. Demonstrated business sense, patience, and tact in dealing with customers. Learned how to motivate low-paid clerical staff by involving them in decisions. (1991)

Entrepreneur, Madison, WI.

Sold mod-logo T-shirts to tourists. Competed with other T-shirt purveyors by choosing the best decals rather than lowering prices. Learned to accept rejection and keep on selling. (1990)

Other: Life guard, golf caddie, library clerk.

Honors: Won Einstein Award for highest grades three times.

Computer Skills: BASIC, Lotus.

Activities: Tutor.

Willing to travel; willing to relocate.

Table 5.3   Examples to validate summary.

Positive Characteristic Conveyed by Summary	Correlated Sentences(s) for Supporting Examples
Innovative	"Established multiethnic food festival . . ."
Good Listener	"Listened to student problems . . ."
Persuasive Presenter	"Persuaded customers to order drinks . . ." "Sold mod-logo T-shirts . . ."
Business Sense	"Learned how various functions . . ." "Demonstrated business sense . . ."
Self-Starter	"Initiated research . . ." "Developed new lay-outs . . ."
Team Builder	"Trained new waiters . . ." "Learned how to motivate . . ."

REVIEW BY THE JOB SEARCH CLUB

The first order of business at our next Job Search Club meeting was to review David's draft résumé. As usual, the Club members had some very interesting comments and questions.

Bill: I'd like to start with David's Summary. Basically, I like it, but I wonder if it's David's best shot. For example, David starts with "Innovative thinking, good listener." That's an accurate description of David, but would that be the most important Positive Characteristic to a Sales Manager?

David: I see what you mean, Bill. I think I was centered on my own preferences rather than being reader-friendly. Maybe I could start with "Persuasive presenter . . . ."

Gabrielle: Following Bill's line of thinking, maybe you should mention your sales experience earlier in your Summary. After all, you're interested in a sales career.

David: That's a good point, Gabrielle. It may make sense to mention the most directly related experience early in the Summary. But I've got to think about that one. My direct sales experience is limited to T-shirts and that was almost three years ago. I don't want to stretch this point. Besides, I did indicate in my Summary that I know the key characteristics of a good salesperson.

I was moderating the meeting, and Alice brought me into the discussion with the next question.

Alice: Richard, both Bill and Gabrielle are asking about the order of statements in the Summary. I'd like to know if the order of Positive Characteristics in the Summary should dictate the order of the validating examples in the text. For example: If David stays with "Innovative thinker . . ." first in his Summary, should he have the example that validates it ("Pig-out with a Pal") first in his Experience section?

Richard: That would be helpful, but don't get tied in knots over it. The value of parallel ordering isn't that great. On the other hand, if something comes first in your Summary, it presumably has a high value. In that case, the validating example also has a high value and should come early in your résumé. There are other factors to consider as well. David is validating most of his message through his Experience section. Still, he is putting his Education section first. On that basis alone, the order of validating examples couldn't parallel exactly the order of Positive Characteristics in the Summary.

Hector: Since David's Experience section is the one that validates most of his Summary, why not put it *before* Education?

Richard: That's a good question. Most career professionals will tell you that you could do it either way. My own recommendation for this point in your life is to put Education first. Let's take David's case as an example. *First,* it tells the employer that you are about to graduate from college. That points the rest of your résumé in an understandable context. *Second,* since David had very good grades, David is telling the employer right away that he has the intellectual capability to do the job. *Third,* David's two sales-related research papers are interesting in themselves and indicate that David's interest in sales didn't begin yesterday. *Fourth,* David's Education section includes a statement about being 60% self-supporting. That statement sends the mini-message that David is mature and self-reliant and that he has done more in college than just have a good time. *Fifth,* the Education section can be read quickly, so it doesn't really slow down the reader in getting to David's Experience.

Alice: What made you put in the subheadings "Academic Semesters" and "Summers"?

David: Remember one of our basic principles, Alice: **A résumé must be logical but it doesn't have to be *chronological*.** I wanted to discuss five jobs, but I didn't want to string them out. By dividing Experience in two parts, I'm giving the reader two chunks.

Robert: But why *those* subheadings, or "chunks," as you called them?

David: That's a good question. This is still a draft, Bob. I'm experimenting with several pairs of chunks, including Private Enterprise/University or

Marketing/Other Fields. I'm not sure yet which rubric I'll use. It will depend on the most logical way to get my message across.

Lauren: I notice that, for each job under Experience, you put the dates at the end.

David: Dates don't have much significance at this point in my career. They're certainly not selling points. Why put them in any earlier?

Robert: David, why did you put your T-shirt experience under the heading "Entrepreneur"? Since you want to go into sales, why not call it "Salesperson"?

David: That's a good question. "Salesperson" might be a good heading for many students with similar experience. But, in my case, I wanted to emphasize business sense and orientation. I think Entrepreneur conveyed that sense better.

Gabrielle: David, I notice that, under Experience, you have a line called "Other." What was your thinking on that?

David: You know, Gabrielle, I've had five jobs in college that help to validate my message. For the sake of completeness, I wanted to mention my other three jobs as well. So I just quickly listed them under "Other." Those three jobs didn't warrant any more space than that.

Lauren: What about your "Activities"?

David: My "Activities" heading is a bit sparse, but that's OK. I've been working 20 to 30 hours a week, so it's clear I do something besides going to class and having a good time.

I didn't want to raise the issue of the Radical Club—it might scare away some employers and it certainly wouldn't attract any. If it comes up at an interview, I won't worry so much. Once they've met me, they'll know that I'm not a wild-eyed bomb thrower. But just looking at "Radical Club" on a résumé might be a turnoff.

A Word to the Wise

David has just made a good point: Everything you write on your résumé must be true. However, you are not obligated to include information that might hurt your chances of winning an interview.

Bill: How about "Willing to travel, willing to relocate"?

David: If I'm going to have a sales career, I'll need to do both of those things. I think it's advantageous to let the employer know that I realize what's required and I'm ready to do it.

LAUREN'S RÉSUMÉ

How did Lauren, whose work experience matched David's, draft her résumé? She proceeded using the same four steps. Because Lauren wanted to be a financial analyst, rather than a salesperson, her résumé was directed to support that objective.

Lauren's first step was to identify the Positive Characteristics she could offer that were important to being a financial analyst. Lauren reviewed available literature and her own informational interviews. Then she identified the Positive Characteristics that she felt she could offer.

Lauren identified this list of Positive Characteristics:

Inquisitive

Analytical

Problem solver

Communication skills

Leadership

Business sense

Self-starter

Lauren made a chart, similar to David's (see Table 5.1), indicating her sources for knowing that these Positive Characteristics were important and why she felt that she could offer them.

LAUREN'S EXAMPLES

Lauren knew that she needed examples to support each Positive Characteristic, for three reasons:

- To make certain she really possessed and could demonstrate each Positive Characteristic;
- To provide material for her résumé text;
- To have an inventory of Positive Characteristics, supported by examples, to help her succeed at her interviews.

Here are a few of the examples Lauren wrote:

Analytical

Demonstrated ability to analyze business issues in accounting class and to interpret the implications of quantitative analysis in finance class.

At Smallco, analyzed cause of receivables backlog and suggested workable solution.

Analyzed cost of materials, risk of tying up limited capital, and price-sensitivity of potential customers, to determine prices for logo T-shirts. (Note: Helped pay for fall tuition.)

We have already discussed David's examples and will not go into further detail about Lauren's. However, it is interesting to compare how David and Lauren described their T-shirt selling experience: Lauren thought in financial terms, and David thought about getting customers.

Variety Is the Spice of Examples

Lauren is demonstrating good sense by writing examples from a variety of sources, including academics, extracurricular activities, and different jobs.

FROM EXAMPLES TO SUMMARY

Lauren was now ready for the third step: determining her message and writing it as a Summary. When Lauren came to see me, we started to discuss her message:

Richard: Lauren, you've completed some important steps you'll need to draft your résumé: You've identified Positive Characteristics that are important to being a financial analyst and that you can offer an employer. Have you thought about the message you want a potential employer to get from reading your résumé, and how you would write your Summary?

Lauren: Yes, Richard, I have. This is what I'm working with: "Combines business education with applied corporate experience. Excellent analytical, problem-solving, and communication skills. Has an inquisitive mind and good business sense."

Richard: Sounds compelling, Lauren. You've started your message with two attractive facts: business education and corporate experience. Neither is an absolute necessity, but both are helpful. I would ask you to think about specifying "finance education"; it quickly establishes a link to being a financial analyst.

Let me ask you about another point: How did you identify analytical, problem-solving, and communication skills as the Positive Characteristics you want to highlight in your Summary?

Lauren: I know that many Positive Characteristics are useful to a financial analyst. The ones I chose were especially emphasized in recruiting literature and by the professionals I interviewed.

Richard: Lauren, I'm a little troubled by the third sentence in your message. You cite "leadership," but I don't see "leadership" in your inventory of examples.

Lauren: My examples gave me some trouble, Richard. Leadership is important, especially if you want to rise from financial *analyst* to financial *manager*. My friends think of me as a leader in our social group. But I never got a title like "President."

Richard: I suggest you rethink that part of your message. Generally, if you don't have a strong, clear example to support a Positive Characteristic, don't make it part of your message.

Remember two points:

- *Nobody* has every desirable Positive Characteristic;
- Don't indicate a Positive Characteristic you can't support with examples. If you *do* get invited to an interview, you may be asked to discuss a Positive Characteristic you don't really have.

After thinking through and clarifying her message, Lauren decided to work with this Summary:

Combines technical finance training with applied corporate experience. Demonstrated skills in writing and presenting. Analytical, inquisitive mind. Seeks to start a career in financial analysis leading to a career in corporate financial management. Interest developed from desire to utilize best talents in a productive career.

Prepared with a Summary that conveyed a well-considered message, Lauren proceeded to draft a text (Education, Experience, Other Selling Points) that would validate her Summary. Let's take a look at each section of Lauren's text.

VALIDATING THROUGH EDUCATION

Lauren wisely decided to identify the Positive Characteristics she wanted to validate in her Education section before proceeding further. This was her initial list:

Positive Characteristic	Validator
Technical finance training	Finance major
Writing	Term papers
Presenting	Oral reports
Analytical, inquisitive skills	(True, but can I validate them here?)

"I have good grades in my finance major," Lauren thought, "and that helps. But what else could I indicate?" The question generated an answer: Lauren had taken more than the required number of accounting courses. That would add validity to *technical finance training*.

"For *writing*, the second point, my research papers on determining lease/ buy decisions and on the role of a manager received good grades. Besides, the first topic will show a technical application of finance principles and the second topic will show a broad interest in management (eventually, I'll be a manager)," Lauren reasoned.

The third Positive Characteristic, *presenting*, might be validated in a number of ways, including formal class reports and presentations made to peers while preparing group assignments. Lauren decided that oral reports could be presented more concisely.

The fourth characteristic, *analytical, inquisitive skills*, was central to Lauren's college education, but difficult to validate with a particular example. "Maybe a third-party testimonial would be useful here," Lauren said to herself. "Noah talked about his 'Righteous Man in His Generation' award. Maybe I could cite my professors' observations of my work."

Lauren now knew what Positive Characteristics she wanted to validate and the examples she would utilize. Based on that preparation, this is what Lauren wrote:

Education:

Emeritus College, Lincoln, NE.

Bachelor of Business Administration, May 1993

Major: Finance (12 credits in Accounting)   Minor: Political Science

Major GPA: 3.3   Overall GPA: 3.2

Research Papers: "Analyzing Relative Risk in Lease/Buy Decisions"; "The Manager's Role in Staff Development."

Oral Presentation: "The Global Impact of Perestroika."

Commended by professors for analytical abilities and inquisitive mind.

Lauren has found a way to utilize her Education section in validating several Positive Characteristics. Lauren may still use her Experience section to validate some of those same Positive Characteristics, if they are important to her message.

ARRANGING EXPERIENCE FOR BEST EFFECT

Lauren knew David well; they had worked together a number of times. She happened to meet David on the campus and eventually they started to discuss their résumés.

David: Lauren, our work histories are so similar, do you want to look at what I wrote for my Experience section?

Lauren: Thanks, David, I'd be glad to look at your résumé. But we're two different people with two different career goals. I think our résumés may look quite different. Why don't we compare notes when we have both completed drafts of our résumés.

Lauren went back to her apartment to work on her Experience section. "What Positive Characteristics am I trying to validate?" she asked herself. This is the list Lauren finally identified:

Positive Characteristic	*Validator*
Applied corporate experience	Smallco Good Buy (retail store)
Presenting	Residence hall counselor
Analytical skills	Smallco Residence Hall? T-shirt?

Lauren realized that her corporate experience would be a major attraction to many employers. Because Smallco was Lauren's most important experience for the purposes of her résumé, she believed her Smallco experience should go first under Experience. But Lauren's most recent job was waiting on tables. To resolve this dilemma, Lauren utilized the same rule David had relied on: **A résumé must be logical but it doesn't have to be chronological.**

Lauren decided to have two subheadings under Experience: Corporate and University. She knew she could align enough experiences under those two subheadings to validate her Positive Characteristics. For the sake of completeness, Lauren could use the rubric of Other to mention her other experiences.

With her basic strategy in mind, Lauren proceeded to draft her Experience section this way:

Experience:

Corporate:

Accounting Assistant, Smallco, Omaha, NE.
Analyzed accounts to determine amount and cause of overaged receivables. Presented a new collections method to senior managers which resulted in 15% increase in monthly revenue.
Learned how to apply finance principles to Smallco's practical needs and the pragmatic challenges of running a profitable business. (Summer 1992)

Associate, Good Buy Department Store, Madison, WI.
Demonstrated tact and patience dealing with customers. Learned about pricing and positioning of products through inquiries to managers and observation of what worked. Reduced Good Buy's tied-up capital by careful monitoring of inventory and ordering practices. (Summer 1991)

University:

Residence Hall Counselor, Emeritus College.
Wrote manual for incoming staff and students about building a healthy community in the Residence Hall. Counseled students on problems ranging from ill-fated romance to ethics. On call 24 hours a day. (Fall 1991–Spring 1992)

Other:

Hustled T-shirts (Summer 1990); Waitperson (Fall 1992–Present)

Lauren compared her text with the Positive Characteristics she had sought to validate. Satisfied that her Experience section had achieved its goal, Lauren came to see me. Lauren and I sat down and engaged in a little verbal sparring.

Richard: Lauren, what if someone said to you that you haven't explained "what you actually did" on these various jobs.
Lauren: I would reply that I had focused on my achievements, namely, what I gave to my employer and what I learned for myself. That

information would be valuable to a future employer. The value of my past history is what it predicts about my future performance. Besides, "One Day in the Life of an Accounting Assistant or Retail Associate" wouldn't be interesting to read.

Richard: That's sound strategy, Lauren. Now let me ask you about some technical points. How did you decide what to italicize and whether to put your job title or the firm's name first?

Lauren: If I had worked for IBM or GE, I would have put the firm's name first because the name of a well-known firm attracts attention and adds stature to my work experience. I chose to put my job title for the Smallco experience first because it has more significance for the reader than my employer's name.

For the sake of consistency, I put all three experiences I discussed in the same format. I used italics as a graphics device to make my résumé easier to read.

Richard: Good thinking, Lauren. I think you made the best choice for your résumé. Still, it would have been acceptable to reverse the order of the job title and firm name. Some students agonize too much about a decision like that.

Under "Other," you put "Hustled T-shirts." What was your thinking about that particular verb?

Lauren: I realized that what I put under "Other" wouldn't make much difference. I mentioned those jobs for the sake of completeness. To the extent that it matters, I chose a verb that would show I was outgoing and assertive.

I personally don't object to using a word like "hustled." However, I do caution students about using words that might convey an offensive meaning to some readers.

OTHER SELLING POINTS

Lauren went to work on the fourth section of her résumé, other selling points (OSP). She determined what her OSPs should be and where on her résumé each OSP belonged.

These are the OSPs Lauren identified, and her thoughts about each one:

Computer skills ("That would reinforce two of my Positive Characteristics, 'technical finance training' and 'analytical.'")

Activities ("My work in the sorority involved leadership. That's always helpful, even if I didn't include it in my Summary.")

Languages ("My Spanish and French would show a multicultural exposure. That can't hurt and it might also reinforce the intellectual curiosity I indicated with 'inquisitive mind.'")

> The OSPs generally add value to your résumé, and I suggest taking them seriously. There's probably more than one "right" place to put them.

After identifying the OSPs she wanted to include in her résumé, Lauren decided where to put them:

Computer skills ("I'll put that under Education. It's a logical place because I learned those skills at Emeritus. Even more important, I want to validate the ability to use my 'technical finance training' efficiently.")

Activities ("Useful, but not critical for me. I'll put this heading after Experience. I was thinking about including it with Education, but that section is getting too crowded.")

> Let's compare how David and Lauren drafted their résumés. Both David and Lauren:
>
> - Used their Summary to convey their message about Positive Characteristics that are important in the profession that is of interest to them;
> - Made communication skills part of their message.
>
> Each had a unique message and Summary. Other differences were:
>
> - Education Section
>   —David utilized it mainly to show that he had gone to college and had received good grades.
>   —Lauren used it to validate several Positive Characteristics.
> - Experience Section
>   —David and Lauren shared five work experiences. However, these common experiences are presented very differently in the two résumés. (Your résumé is a *presentation of you,* not a series of job descriptions.)
>   —David used "Summer/Academic Year" subheadings; Lauren used "Corporate/University."

Figure 5.2 Lauren's draft résumé.

Lauren Appleman

Current Address: *Permanent Address*
2469 Cornhusker Court   1359 Loco Parent's Place
Lincoln, NE 68540   Madison, WI 53722

Summary: Combines technical finance training with applied corporate experience. Demonstrated skills in writing and presenting. Analytical, inquisitive mind. Seeks to start a career in financial analysis leading to a career in corporate financial management. Interest developed from desire to utilize best talents in a productive career.

Education: Emeritus College, Lincoln, NE.

Bachelor of Business Administration, May 1993

Major: Finance (12 credits in Accounting)   Minor: Political Science
Major GPA: 3.3   Overall GPA: 3.2
Research Papers: "Analyzing Relative Risk in Lease/Buy Decisions"
                          "The Manager's Role in Staff Development"
Oral Presentation: "The Global Impact of Perestroika"
Computer Skills: BASIC, Pascal, Lotus, Dbase.

Commended by professors for analytical abilities and inquisitive mind.

Experience:

Corporate:

Accounting Assistant, Smallco, Omaha, NE.

Analyzed receivables to determine amount and cause of overaged receivables. Presented a new collections method to senior managers which resulted in 15% increase in monthly revenue.

Learned how to apply finance principles to Smallco's practical needs and the pragmatic challenges of running a profitable business. (Summer 1992)

Associate, Good Buy Department Store, Madison, WI.
Demonstrated tact and patience dealing with customers. Learned about pricing and positioning of products through inquiries to managers and observation of what worked. Reduced Good Buy's tied-up capital by careful monitoring of inventory and ordering   practices. (Summer 1991)

University:

Residence Hall Counselor, Emeritus College.
Wrote manual for incoming staff and students about building a healthy community in the Residence Hall.

Counseled students on problems ranging from ill-fated romance to ethics. On call 24 hours a day. (Fall, 1991–Spring, 1992)

Other: Hustled T-shirts (Summer 1990); Waitperson. (Fall 1991–Present)

Languages: Conversant in Spanish and French.

Activities: Elected Member: Residence Council
Treasurer: Alpha Beta Gamma Sorority

Willing to travel; willing to relocate

References available upon request.

Languages ("Has about the same importance for my prospective employer as my activities, especially since I'm conversant in Spanish and French, but not really fluent.")

Lauren finished the four sections of her résumé (Summary, Education, Experience, Other Selling Points) and put them together in the draft shown in Figure 5.2.

WHERE ARE ALL THE SAMPLE RÉSUMÉS?

Some books designed to help you find a good job include many model résumés for you to look at and follow. This book gives you several samples,* but not page after page of résumés. Here's why:

- My goal is to teach you a *process* that you can use to write your own winning résumé. By following my process, you will:
  —Understand better the value you can contribute to your next employer;
  —Present yourself in a résumé that will earn you more interviews;
  —Be ready to write different résumés for different situations now and in the future.

> A good way to test your résumé is to ask someone who hardly knows you to read it and then to describe you, based on your résumé. If the description given of you is close to the message you wanted to convey, you have written your résumé well.

In this chapter, we have seen how two students in our Job Search Club, Lauren and David, went through the process of writing a résumé. Both developed a message indicating the Positive Characteristics that would make their applications attractive to a potential employer. Their messages were conveyed by a Summary and validated by the other three sections of their résumé (Experience, Education, Other Selling Points).

David and Lauren had five work experiences in common, yet they wrote two substantially different résumés. They are two different people with two different career goals.

In the next two chapters, we will move on to another step in your job search: your cover letter and outreach campaign.

---

* Samples are not models. The samples show you some possible results of using my process, but they should not be followed blindly. The process in this book may lead you to a good résumé that is different from those you have seen in this book.

PART THREE

Finding an Employer

CHAPTER SIX

Cover Letters

Cover letters serve three main purposes for a prospective employer. First, they tell your readers whether you can write. Because written communication is important to American business, a poorly executed letter will implicitly say you can't write and will damage your chances severely. A well-written letter is a point in your favor. In addition, cover letters are indicative of how serious you are in applying to a particular firm. If you seem serious, maybe you'll get an interview; if you're not serious, you definitely won't. Finally, cover letters should tell employers something about you that they might not learn from your résumé. In this way, they can benefit both you and the persons reading your letter.

PURPOSE AND VALUE TO YOU

For you, the job applicant, your cover letter has *one main purpose:* to help get you invited to a job interview. By tailoring your communication to the interests of the addressee firm, you can add value to your résumé in any of three ways:

1. You *highlight* Positive Characteristics that are of particular interest to the reader. Although these characteristics are probably conveyed in your résumé, your cover letter offers you the opportunity to give them the prominence and emphasis you want for a particular situation.
2. You can *reframe* items from your résumé to address the particular interests of your potential employer.
3. You can introduce *new material* that is of specific interest to an employer and that might be very difficult or awkward to include in a résumé.

Examples of highlighting, reframing, and new material will be given throughout this chapter.

MODULAR CONSTRUCTION

Writing cover letters can be time-consuming. Most people don't consider writing business letters fun. To make the best use of your time and to make your effort as painless as possible, I suggest building a *prototype* letter that can serve as the source for all your cover letters. When you've written your first letter, you have then written the rest.

You should write four core paragraphs that cover these topics:

- Your purpose for writing;
- Your Positive Characteristics that would be of interest to the employer;
- Why you want the job;
- The next step after receipt of your résumé.

Each paragraph will contain several sentences or modules. Once you have written your prototype letter, you can move or modify an existing module or introduce a new one.

Let's look at your four core paragraphs one at a time. Your first paragraph will have between two and four sentences and will quickly convey the following information to the reader:

- What you are *writing about*—presumably, your interest in a particular type of job or a specific "training program";
- How your *interest* in that field or position developed;
- Your *academic credentials*, if they are a clear selling point (for example, Bachelor of Business Arts in Accounting, Bachelor of Arts from a prestigious college, or Honors student);

> Remember, you have an Education section in your résumé. A simple mention of your graduation is often sufficient in a cover letter.

- An indication that your past *work experience* is of value to this employer (if true).

Your first paragraph might be worded like this:

I am interested in joining Sundance Marketing, Inc., as a sales representative. My interest in sales has developed from both my work experience and my college courses in business.

Your second paragraph will highlight the Positive Characteristics that you feel are of particular interest to that employer. You may use either a standard paragraph format or a bullet format. I prefer the bullet format because it is easier to type, easier to read, and easier to modify for the next letter. However, format is a matter of style, and the choice is yours.

Here's an example of the bullet format for your second paragraph:

I am certain that I would be an asset to your firm. Among the attributes I offer are:

- *Two summers of sales experience*—financed most of tuition from commission-based jobs;
- *Thorough knowledge of your product*—I have been an avid widget user for years;
- *Excellent communication and persuasion skills*—demonstrated in both work and academic situations;
- *Maturity and sense of direction*—I started college only after determining my goals and serving three years in the U.S. Army. [For other students: . . . after two years of productive experience in business.]

These same Positive Characteristics could be conveyed in paragraph form.

Your third paragraph will explain why you want to work for that firm. If possible, address both the type of job and your impression of the firm. In most cases, you should also explain your attraction to the industry and to the geographic location in which you would be working. Citing something you have read about the firm in either the general press or a trade publication can be very helpful. Your third paragraph might look like this:

A position in finance with Toolco would be very appealing to me, for several reasons. *First,* I am eager to build a career in a field where I can utilize my skills in analysis, research, and communication. *Second,* I am attracted to the manufacturing sector because it is the real growth sector of business in America. *Third,* I am especially excited about Toolco. Your firm was recently described in *The Wall Street Journal* as "an innovative, medium-sized company where the creativity, hard work and dedication of its employees have resulted in exceptional growth and outstanding growth potential." Toolco has the kind of working environment I want to be a part of. *Fourth,* I know that Toolco expects its people to move around the several divisions of the company. I would enjoy starting my career in your St. Louis headquarters and I'm ready to relocate as necessary.

Your *fourth* paragraph closes your letter with an expression of what you expect will happen next:

I am eager to meet with you to discuss career possibilities for me at Toolco. Next week, I will call your office to see when a meeting can be arranged.

Sincerely yours,

Your Name

Enclosure: Résumé

Your last paragraph will be polite but to the point. Notice that *you* will take the initiative to call the firm. This makes sense, for at least two reasons:

- Your call keeps the initiative in your hands and eases the employer's burden of responding. Both of these outcomes increase, however marginally, your probability of being invited to a job interview.
- Your call shows more than average interest in the position. Evidence of interest cannot hurt you.

When the four paragraphs are put together, your prototype cover letter might look like the one shown as Figure 6.1. It was written by a subcommittee of our Job Search Club, using the pseudonym Isaiah Amoson.

A cover letter should add value to a résumé; otherwise, all it says is "Dear Employer, here is my résumé." Table 6.1 shows whether Isaiah's prototype has done its job.

After examining the value added column, the Job Search Club agreed that Isaiah's cover letter had done its job.

MODIFYING YOUR LETTER

Let's look at some examples of how to modify a prototype cover letter to fit a particular situation. In this case, the JSC looked at applying to Smartbuy, a regional retailer.

Lauren: Isaiah gave three reasons why he wanted to work for Prophetco. I like his strategy for Smartbuy as well, but now we have to change the details. In terms of Isaiah's first point, *attraction to the industry,* he might want to say something like this:

Figure 6.1　Sample cover letter—subcommittee project.

70 Admonition Avenue
Lincoln, NE 68542
October 10, 1992

Ms. Miriam Hanavi
Vice President, Marketing
Prophetco
249 Alderman Avenue
Chicago, IL 60616

Dear Ms. Hanavi:

I am interested in joining Prophetco as a marketing analyst. My interest in marketing has developed in part from my academic coursework relating to this field. In addition, I worked my way through college in jobs that enabled me to see both the professional marketer and the American consumer in action.

I am certain that I will be an asset to Prophetco. Among the attributes I offer are:

- *Technical training*—critical skills like statistics, psychology, and marketing;
- *Related experience*—during two summers in the retail industry, I increased sales by analyzing customer demand and arranging displays accordingly;
- *Clear sense of professional direction*—I have been investigating a career as a market analyst through meetings with professionals and reading the appropriate trade literature;
- *Research and writing skills*—demonstrated in research papers that have averaged A– throughout college;
- *Knowledge of Prophetco's products*—I have used "Foresight," "Repentance," and "Redemption" with an avid interest.

A market analyst position at Prophetco would be very appealing to me, for several reasons. First, I am attracted to spiritually oriented consumer products in general. I believe the spiritual products industry plays an important social role. Second, I am impressed by Prophetco's growth potential in particular. As the *Spiritual Advisor Press* recently reported: "Prophetco has both the best products and the best business plan in the industry." Third, I grew up in the Midwest and still have many friends in the Chicago area. Therefore, working for Prophetco would be more like coming home than relocating.

I am eager to meet with you in person, to discuss career possibilities for me at Prophetco. I'll be in Chicago early next month, and that would provide an excellent opportunity for me to come to your office without incurring travel expenses. Next week, I will call you to see when a meeting can be arranged.

Sincerely yours,

Isaiah Amoson

Enclosure: Résumé

Table 6.1   Cover letter as a complement to a résumé.

Paragraph	Value Added
First	Explains the letter's purpose. This paragraph may highlight some material covered in the résumé's Summary. A sentence like ". . . jobs that enabled me to see both the professional marketer and the American consumer . . ." reframes material from the résumé's Experience section to make it more directly related to a particular employer—Prophetco, in this case.
Second	*Technical training:* Identifying courses reframes part of résumé's Education section and highlights knowledge of areas related to being a marketing analyst. Often a good idea in a cover letter but awkward in a résumé.
	Related experience: Highlights work experience most connected to being a marketing analyst.
	Clear sense of professional direction: Introduces something important that is not on résumé. This kind of statement could also be the third part of the Summary statement on the résumé.
	Research and writing skills: Reframes research papers information on résumé; shows *competence* rather than specific areas of research.
	Knowledge of company's products: New information that helps to tailor the letter to a specific firm.
Third	A description like ". . . attracted to spiritually oriented products" shows an avocational interest in addition to a purely professional one.
	". . . I am impressed by Prophetco's growth potential" is tailored to Prophetco by showing specific research of firm.
	". . . I grew up in the Midwest" minimizes doubts about social problems or a refusal to relocate. Often, it is a good idea to allay the employer's doubts about your mental preparation. This would include relocation, if your college is not near the firm you're writing to.
Fourth	The message here is "I'll take the initiative in making and sustaining contact."

First, I am attracted to the retail industry because I enjoy the challenge of constant decisions about products, prices, and displays.

David: To follow up on Lauren's idea, Isaiah should make his second point his *attraction to Smartbuy in particular.* He might say something like this:

The Short Letter

Is there a situation where you don't need a cover letter with your résumé? Yes: when you are handing your résumé to someone face-to-face. This often occurs at a Job Fair.

It's still a good idea to follow up with a letter to the person you met. A *short* letter is sufficient because you have already introduced yourself in person.

Your letter will serve two purposes. It will reinforce your statement of interest in the firm, and it will call extra attention to *your* résumé from among the many collected at the Job Fair.

864 Integrity Drive
Lincoln, NE 68550
October 20, 1992

Mr. Charles Powell
Senior Recruiter
Foresight Optical, Inc.
17 Vision Road
Omaha, NE 68139

Dear Mr. Powell:

It was a pleasure meeting you at the Emeritus College Job Fair on October 15. I appreciated the opportunity to learn more about Foresight Optical and the career opportunities possible with your firm.

As we discussed at the Job Fair, I have an interest in marketing industrial products such as the lenses manufactured by Foresight.

For your convenience, I have enclosed another copy of my résumé. I will call you next week to discuss what our next step should be.

Sincerely,

Gabrielle Finnerty

Enclosure: Résumé

Second, I am particularly attracted to Smartbuy because of its success in meeting market trends and its policy of involving employees in decision making.

Hector: If we stick with Isaiah's strategy in the prototype, he should try to *allay a possible concern* the employer might have about Isaiah's mental preparation for the job. Maybe Isaiah could address the "long hours, low glamour" reality:

Third, I enjoy a job that offers variety, growth, and a chance to see results. I don't mind long hours and I don't expect glamour.

A Typical Modification?

When you review the changes made to Isaiah's prototype by the JSC (see Figure 6.2), you might feel that quite a bit of massaging or modifying was necessary. There are a few points to remember:

- Isaiah's prototype made his Smartbuy letter much easier by:
  —Laying out his basic cover letter strategy;
  —Identifying modules to be massaged (modified), moved, or inserted.
  —Providing at least some of the text for the Smartbuy letter.
- The changes were relatively numerous because Isaiah's Smartbuy letter differed from his prototype in terms of both industry and job function. If either had remained the same, fewer changes would have been necessary.
- The Smartbuy letter now becomes Isaiah's prototype cover letter for the retail industry.

No matter how many changes Isaiah made, his prototype made his Smartbuy letter easier and less time-consuming to write.

Taking the suggestions of the JSC members, Isaiah's letter to Smartbuy was revised, as shown in Figure 6.2.

In this chapter, we have learned how to construct a four-paragraph prototype cover letter. We have seen the purpose of each paragraph and how to massage the prototype to create a cover letter to a specific firm.

Now that we are getting into the swing of writing cover letters, let's see how the Job Search Club determined why and when to write them, in an activity called Outreach.

Figure 6.2 Sample cover letter revised for new recipient.

70 Admonition Avenue
Lincoln, NE 68542
October 24, 1992

Mr. Edward Bargain
Vice President, Retailing
Smartbuy, Inc.
975 Tire Road
Dayton, OH 45443

Dear Mr. Bargain:

I am interested in building a career with Smartbuy in store management. My interest in this field has developed from my retail store experience and my coursework at Emeritus College, from which I will graduate in May, 1993.

I am certain that I will be an asset to Smartbuy. Among the attributes I offer are:

- *Retail experience* —two summers of learning, first-hand, everything from product displays to customer relations;
- *Business sense* —ability to identify and respond quickly to pragmatic dollar-and-cents situations;
- *Leadership and organizing abilities* —demonstrated as vice president of college ski club, for which I organized many trips and a membership drive;
- *Clear sense of professional direction* —I have been investigating a career in the retail industry through meetings with retail professionals and staying current with the trade literature;
- *Knowledge of Smartbuy's strategy:* I have experienced your approach to the cost-conscious consumer as a frequent shopper and unofficial product watcher. In addition, I have read about Smartbuy in *Business Week* and *The Wall Street Journal.*

A career in store management, beginning in your Executive Training Program, would be very appealing to me, for several reasons. *First,* I am attracted to the retail industry because I enjoy the challenge of constant decisions about products, prices, and displays. *Second,* I am attracted to Smartbuy in particular because of your success in meeting market trends and your policy of involving employees in decision making. *Third,* I enjoy a job that offers variety, growth, and a chance to see results. I don't mind long hours and I don't expect glamour.

I am eager to meet with you in person, to discuss career possibilities for me at Smartbuy. I am familiar with the Dayton area; I spent four years there when my mother worked for NCR. Next week, I will call you to see when a meeting can be arranged.

Sincerely,

Isaiah Amoson

Enclosure: Résumé

CHAPTER SEVEN

Outreach

In this chapter, we will identify the benefits of an outreach campaign, learn how to build sources of contacts, and simulate your follow-up to arrange interviews.

EXPANDING YOUR OPPORTUNITIES

At the next meeting of the Job Search Club, we discussed outreach.

Lauren: What does outreach mean exactly? Why should we conduct an outreach campaign?

Richard: Outreach means that you take the initiative to contact prospective employers, requesting a job interview. There are three major reasons for conducting an Outreach Campaign. I call them the Outreach Trilogy.

Gabrielle (indicating some concern): I'm a little intimidated by the fact that there are thousands of firms in America. How can we access them?

Richard: Gabrielle, let's see if we can come up with a list of outreach sources. Who has some ideas?

Discussing Outreach together, the membership of our JSC identified nine good sources for building an outreach list.

Hector: My question is similar to Gabrielle's. Why didn't we include Help Wanted advertisements in our list of Outreach sources?

Richard: Help Wanted ads should be put into perspective:

- *Most jobs are never advertised;* some authors estimate that 85 percent of all job openings are not advertised.
- Jobs that are advertised are *usually for experienced hires,* not recent college grads.

The Outreach Trilogy

There are three reasons why conducting an outreach campaign makes good sense:

- You *increase your options.* A moderate-size recruiting program includes about 150 firms. Some colleges have more firms visiting their campuses, but many colleges have fewer. There are *thousands* of good firms in America. You shouldn't ignore the largest block of potential employers.
- You can tap the *big market of small businesses.* Many employers hire recent college grads, but don't recruit on any campus, anywhere. This is especially true of small and medium-size firms. Yet, *in the aggregate,* small and medium-size firms employ a large and growing section of the labor market. Why cut yourself out of an entire range of employment opportunities?
- You gain *peace of mind.* If you don't conduct an outreach campaign, you're likely to wonder what opportunities you missed. Initiating contacts with employers, even if they don't yield interviews or job offers, can at least add to your knowledge that you tried.

Sources for Outreach

This is a summary of the sources for an outreach list identified by our Job Search Club:

- Alumni Magazine—references to "Where They Are Now."
- Alumni Mentors—available through the college.
- Business stories in the general and business-oriented press.
- Chambers of Commerce.
- College Placement Council Annual. (a guide to employment opportunities for college graduates)
- Practicing professionals—connections from informational meetings.
- Professional Associations.
- Regional Business Magazines
- Specialized Career Books

- Advertised jobs that are addressed to recent college grads are *usually very low-level.* In addition, jobs titled "college graduates" or "management trainees" are often misleading to the reader because they refer to straight-commission sales jobs.
- Applicants face *lopsided odds.* Jobs that are advertised tend to get a much larger response than jobs that are not advertised. The sheer volume of mailed-in résumés diminishes your chance for an interview.

For these reasons, I wouldn't rely on Help Wanted ads as my *main* source for interviews.

WHO GETS YOUR LETTER?

Alice: Richard, so far, we've been talking mostly about sourcing the names of companies that might fit our professional goals and geographic preferences. How do we find the names of the best *person* to write to?

Richard: I recommend writing to the *highest authority* in the company who has the *power to hire* people in your field of interest. For example, since you're interested in public accounting, you could write to the firm's Partner-in-Charge. Hector is interested in corporate finance, so he might write to a firm's Chief Financial Officer.

David: But won't these big shots just kick our letters down to some subordinate or to personnel?

Richard: Probably, but let me tell you why I have given you this advice:

- All "shots," big or small, are human beings, not deities. You have every right to write to anybody you want.
- It's often easier to get the name of a high official than a lower official. Writing to the Chief Financial Officer, for example, can actually save you research time.
- Even if your letter is "kicked down," you have lost nothing and gained something. For example, if your letter gets referred to personnel, you're no worse off than if you had written to the personnel office directly. You may be *better off* because your letter will come with a buckslip from the CFO or whomever. Buckslips from powerful people grab attention.

IDENTIFYING INDIVIDUALS

Gabrielle: Richard, I can understand writing to the highest ranking official in the functional area of interest to us. But how can we get those names?

Richard: Gabrielle, let's see what ideas your fellow members of the JSC can suggest.

Six Outreach Steps

At Bill's request, I summarized for the JSC my six outreach steps:

1. *Identify the profession(s).* Through your work in "Finding Out," you may have identified at least one career you want to pursue. Perhaps you identified three; that's OK. You only have a problem if the number of professions that interest you is zero or 50.
2. *Identify your geographic preference.* Most students prefer some area of the country over others. Typical criteria are:

   Where you *grew up;*

   Where you went to *college;*

   Where your *Significant Other* lives (consider the implications of your commitment both for yourself and for the other person);

   Someplace exciting, based on image (California, New York, Boston) and reputed status as a singles' heaven;

   Where the jobs are, because some areas of the country are more prosperous than others at any given moment (but would you like to live there?);

3. *Identify firms,* using nine sources we have already identified;
4. *Identify individuals,* using the approach the JSC discussed earlier (we'll discuss the pragmatics shortly);
5. *Send your cover letters and résumés;*
6. *Follow up each letter* until you have a clear answer about being invited to a job interview.

Robert: There are some readily available sources in our reference room. For example, *Hoover's Profiles of Over 500 Major Corporations* gives about two pages of information on each of the 500 firms. The information includes the names of the senior officers. It also includes good information about the firm that might help you with your cover letter.

Another available source is *annual reports.* If the firm is publicly held, it must issue a financial summary of the year's activities. At Emeritus, we have a current file of annual reports in our reference room. Besides giving the names of the officers, the annual report gives information about the firm you could use in your cover letter. You can also call the firm and ask for the name of the Chief Financial Officer or the Director of Marketing.

FOLLOWING UP

Lauren: I'd like to discuss in more detail the last of the six outreach steps: Follow up. Richard, could you walk us through an example of a follow-up?

Richard: OK, Lauren; that's a good idea. But let's do a quick review of the other five steps first. Let's say you've identified Carol Jackson, Vice President of Finance, at Widgetco in Memphis, Tennessee, as the person you are writing to. This assumes you have identified a profession of interest to you (step 1), identified a geographic preference (step 2), identified a firm of interest (step 3), and identified Carol as the highest ranking official in the functional area of interest to you—in this case, finance (step 4). You have modified your prototype cover letter to highlight Positive Characteristics that are of specific interest to Widgetco and sent off your letter (step 5).

I suggest calling after one week. It's easier to keep track of the connection between your letters and calls in that time frame, and one week is plenty of time for your letter to arrive.

Bill: I'm trying to picture the situation. Lauren mails her letter to Carol Jackson on October 1. Now it's October 8. Lauren calls Widgetco and says, "Is my dear friend Vice President Carol Jackson in?"

Bill was making a good point in a humorous way. It's not easy to call a prospective employer under any circumstances, and calling a vice president can feel especially intimidating. But with a little preparation, you can do it.

CALLING THE HEAD HONCHO

Richard: Lauren, why don't you and I role-play your call to Carol Jackson?

Lauren: OK. Ding-a-ling.

[So far, just like calling a friend.]

"Widgetco Operator": Good morning; Widgetco.

Lauren: I'd like to speak with Carol Jackson, please.

[Usually, the switchboard receptionist doesn't ask too many questions.]

"Secretary": Carol Jackson's office. Good morning.

Lauren: I'd like to speak with Carol Jackson, please. Is she in?

"Secretary": Who's calling please, and what is this in reference to?

Lauren: This is Lauren Appelman. I'm following up on my letter of October 1.

"Secretary": Is this in reference to a job?

[Hint: Don't lie!]

Lauren: Yes, it is. My letter to Ms. Jackson explained my interest in a finance career at Widgetco.

"Secretary": All correspondence of that type is referred to Dan Chaney in personnel. I'll transfer you to that office.

Time-out from the role-play. In this scenario, Lauren didn't get a chance to speak with Carol Jackson. Should she feel discouraged? No! She is no worse off than if she had written Dan Chaney directly. Perhaps Carol Jackson's buckslip on top of Lauren's cover letter and résumé will even help.

"Personnel Secretary": This is Mr. Chaney's office. Good morning.

Lauren: Good morning. This is Lauren Appelman. Is Dan Chaney available?

"Personnel Secretary": Is he expecting your call?

[Remember: Don't lie!]

Lauren: Carol Jackson's office referred me to Mr. Chaney.

"Personnel Secretary": Is this in regard to a job?

[*Hint:* Keep your cool. It's true you just answered that question, but you were speaking to someone else.]

Lauren: Yes, it is. In my letter to Ms. Jackson, I explained my interest in building a career in finance at Widgetco.

"Personnel Secretary": When did you send your letter?

Lauren: October 1.

"Personnel Secretary": Well, we do respond to all résumés. You should be hearing from us soon.

Lauren: I understand. However, please let Mr. Chaney know that I called. He may want to ask me a few questions about my letter to Carol Jackson.

"Personnel Secretary": Do you know Ms. Jackson?

[*Hint:* Don't lie; but you can tell the truth in a constructive way.]

Lauren: I hope you understand that I prefer not to discuss my relationship to Ms. Jackson right now.

This statement is true—and it may leave the secretary concerned about a *possible* connection to Carol Jackson. This increases the probability that the secretary will bring your message to Dan Chaney's attention.

WHAT LAUREN GAINED

Gabrielle: That was an interesting role-play dialogue you just had with Lauren. But what did Lauren gain from it?

Richard: Gabrielle, I'd say that Lauren gained three things. *First,* she now knows who has her résumé. *Second,* she has called extra attention to her résumé twice: by the vice president's buckslip and by her message to Dan Chaney. *Third,* Lauren can benefit psychologically because she has kept the initiative in her own hands.

Bill: I'd like to ask about that third part. Is the initiative really in Lauren's hands? After all, according to the secretary, it seems Lauren will just have to wait until Dan Chaney gets back to her.

Richard: I'm glad you followed up on that point, Bill. Actually, Lauren doesn't have to just wait by her mailbox for a letter from Widgetco. I suggest that Lauren call Dan Chaney again, in another week. At that time, Lauren could say something like this when she's connected to Dan Chaney's secretary: "Good morning. This is Lauren Appelman calling, to follow up on our conversation of last week. I wonder if there have been any developments on my request for an interview?"

David: Do you think Lauren will really get an answer? Besides, if she keeps calling, won't she just irritate Dan Chaney?

Richard: You've asked two good questions, David, but they're really related. I don't know whether Lauren will get an answer. I *do know* that, if she calls once a week in a professional and courteous manner, she will *not hurt* her chances any *and* her expression of more-than-average interest in getting an interview may help her achieve that goal. Lauren has nothing to lose and something to gain in terms of getting an interview. *Polite persistence* is a no-lose approach.

WHEN THE BIG WHEEL COMES TO THE PHONE

So far, the JSC had been speaking about the possibility (actually, the probability) of not being connected to the person the cover letter had been addressed to. But what if Carol Jackson or Dan Chaney answers the phone?

Alice: Richard, let's be optimistic. Let's say the vice president, Carol Jackson, *does* answer Lauren's call. I've never spoken to a corporate vice president. What should we say?

Richard: Alice, most people find it hard to ask a stranger for something, especially over the phone. It's even harder to speak to a person who has substantial authority.

First, you should accept the fact that you're going to be nervous. Everybody is. Second, remember that Carol Jackson is just a human being who holds an important position. She's human and you're human. Besides, you need a good job, and vice presidents need a good staff. You may really need each other.

Alice: OK; but let's say I call Widgetco and Carol Jackson does answer the phone. Can we role-play that conversation?

Richard: I think that would benefit everyone.

Alice: Good morning. This is Alice Perugia. Is Carol Jackson in?

"Carol Jackson":   This is Carol Jackson. May I help you?

Alice: Ms. Jackson, I wrote to you on October 1, explaining my interest in a finance career at Widgetco. I hope you have received my letter.

"Carol Jackson":   I'm not sure. What did your letter say?

"Semper Paratus" ("Always Be Prepared")

Applicants should be prepared for this question. In fact, Alice has just been given a great opening. Alice can now paraphrase her letter, indicating what Alice can give Widgetco and why she wants to build a career in finance there.

Alice: [Brief explanation of the second and third paragraphs of her letter.]

"Carol Jackson":   That sounds very interesting. Yes, I'd like to speak with you.

Applicants should be prepared for this opportunity, too, and should not hesitate to suggest a meeting time.

Alice: I plan to be in Memphis from November 4 to 6. Tuesday morning, November 5, would be best for me, but I can come on any of those three days.

"Carol Jackson":   How about Wednesday, November 6, at 2:00 P.M.?

[*Hint:* You have hooked the fish. Don't quibble about details.]

Alice: That's great, Ms. Jackson. Wednesday, November 6, at 2:00 P.M. I look forward to seeing you then.

Alice noted her interview appointment on her calendar and wrote a short letter to Carol Jackson to express her pleasure at speaking with Ms. Jackson that morning, to confirm the appointment, and to indicate that she looked forward to meeting Ms. Jackson in person.

A NOTE ON ETIQUETTE

Lauren: How should we be referring to and addressing the people we want to speak with?

Richard: This is what I suggest. When speaking to someone you have never actually met, be on the safe side. Ask to speak with "Dan Chaney," rather than "Dan," for example. When the person you've written to is on the phone, use "Ms." or "Mr."—"Ms. Jackson" rather than "Carol."

After you have met a person, or during an interview, it is generally acceptable (and sometimes even preferable) to refer to the other person by his or her first name.

LOGISTICS

Hector, our future CFO, wanted to clarify the budget items for an outreach campaign. I gave him my Outreach Logistics Planner (OLP) to examine.

Outreach Logistics Planner (OLP)

These are the elements you need to take into account in your outreach campaign.

To arrange an interview

Time: research on firms and people; massaging your cover letter and résumé; placing follow-up calls.

Money: postage and phone calls.

After an interview is arranged

Time: prepare for interview; travel to and from interview site.

Money: travel expenses; wardrobe (but see the Dress Is Critical Myth, in Chapter 9.)

Hector: These time-and-money items could amount to a bundle of cash. Are there any ways to save on some of these expenses?

Richard: Here are a few money-saving tips that are worth trying:

- Call the "800" information operator. Some businesses have "800" numbers available for use.
- If you need to travel,
  —Try to schedule your visits for a time when you would be in or near the firm's city anyway.
  —Try to arrange *several* interviews during each trip to a particular place.
  —Try to stay with friends or relatives, to save hotel costs.
- Remember: Almost always, *you* will be responsible for travel expenses to an initial interview.

WILL YOUR HEAD BE HUNTED?

Before the meeting of the JSC adjourned, Gabrielle asked me about specialized employment agencies—headhunters, as some people call them. I strongly discourage approaching headhunters, for two reasons:

- *They usually can't help you;* they tend to place experienced professionals, not recent college graduates;
- Some headhunters can hurt you by deflating your self-esteem.

In this chapter, we have seen how and why to conduct an outreach campaign, including identifying contacts and following up to arrange interviews.

The next Part of the book deals with interviews—how to prepare for them and succeed at them.

PART FOUR

Interviewing

CHAPTER EIGHT

Preparing

The topic of this chapter, preparing for an interview, covers the first of five steps in a successful interview. Subsequent chapters will cover axing anxiety (debunking the great interview myths), promoting your Positive Characteristics; asking productive questions, and asking for the job. The final chapter in Part Four takes you along as Lauren is interviewed for the first time as a prospective business professional.

Usually, an initial interview with a firm is a screening interview. The firm's main goal is to identify individuals it would like to invite for a Site Visit, a second interview, or a similar advanced screening. Whether your initial interview is held on-campus or at the firm's office, the procedure will be the same.

You are not likely to be offered a professional job at an initial interview. Success at your initial interview means being invited to a Site Visit, which is a step toward a job offer, your ultimate goal in the interview process.

If you follow my advice in this chapter, you will benefit in five ways:

1. You will be able to answer the two most central themes of a typical interview: Why should we hire you? Why do you want to work for us?
2. You will be able to answer the frequently asked question: "Tell me what you know about our company."
3. You will convince your interviewer that you are truly interested in his or her firm and that you come prepared to meetings.
4. You will be more successful with the questions you ask at your interview.
5. You will allay a good deal of your own interview anxiety because you will *know* you are well-prepared.

THE TWIN PEAKS OF INTERVIEWING

Running through your entire interview will be questions focused on two basic themes, which I call the twin peaks of interviewing:

Ten Principles of Interviewing

These are the interviewing principles I teach my students. Review them frequently as you go through the interviewing process.

1. An interview is a *business meeting between equals.* Both you and your interviewer have business objectives: The firm wants to hire good employees; you want a good job. The interviewer is not an all-powerful corporate giant who holds your fate in his or her hands, and you are not "a kid" or "just a student." You want a good job; the company wants a good employee. The situation is perfectly balanced.

2. *Always put in; never put on.* A key to interviewing success is the preparation you *put in* before each interview; you cannot compensate for lack of preparation by *putting on* behavior designed to con or psych-out your interviewer.

3. *Don't worry! What's the worst that can happen?* Ax your anxiety by putting your worries in the proper perspective and focusing on a constructive outlook.

4. *Be yourself at your best.* No one else can be you, and you can't succeed if you try to pretend you're someone else. Besides, the firm invited *you* to the interview. Let the best of you—the major part of the real you—come out.

5. *Let the good things in your past predict your future.* Your past is neither a straitjacket limiting you nor a golden passport guaranteeing success. You will give your future employer some of the benefits you have given to past employers, co-workers, and social acquaintances.

6. *Promote your Positive Characteristics;* no one else will. Your Positive Characteristics will impress employers if they are believably the way you are.

7. *Dress without distress.* This year's power tie or "in" hemline won't get you hired.

8. *Focus on your purpose: getting a job offer.* Direct all your energy toward that objective.

9. *Don't think about your competition.* Focus only on things you can influence, such as the quality of your own preparation.

10. *Internalize—don't memorize.* Study but don't try to memorize these principles or your responses before an interview. Let the principles and your responses become a part of you that comes out naturally during an interview. If you memorize, your interviewer will know it and won't see you as a professional at a business meeting.

- Why should we hire you?
- Why do you want to work for us?

Let's take a look at the first peak. When you were writing your résumé, I suggested that you bring out the Positive Characteristics that would be important to a prospective employer. Because of your good résumé, you were invited to an interview. Those same Positive Characteristics must now be put on display during the interview. You may need to make some modifications because you will be interviewing with a particular firm about a particular job.

Alice, an accounting major, was very excited when she came to see me in October of her senior year. A very high academic achiever, Alice had earned interviews with most of the accounting firms to which she had applied. Could she succeed with the next, dreaded step—her interviews?

Why Should We Hire You?

To prepare an answer for "Why should we hire you?" seemed like a daunting challenge. Alice felt that there was so much to say but so little she could articulate.

Alice and I sat down to discuss an approach to this question. Because her first interview would be with Sincere & Olde, a prominent public accounting firm, we decided to focus on that interview. My first step was to help Alice organize the material she was learning so that the information in it was readily available for both immediate use and the later stages in her job search process. Building on her informational interviews and résumé preparation, I suggested that Alice needed to identify:

- What was important to public accounting firms in general;
- What was important to Sincere & Olde in particular;
- What examples would show that Alice had those attributes.

Based on her previous research, Alice prepared a "Why You Should Hire Me" (WYSHM) chart. An abbreviated version is shown as Table 8.1.

Although Alice's chart needed some fine-tuning, she was now in a position to answer the question "Why Should We Hire You?" I role-played a Sincere & Olde interview when Alice showed me her chart.

"Interviewer": Alice, I was very impressed by your résumé. That's why I decided to interview you. Why do you think S & O should want to hire you?

Alice: (pauses for a moment to collect her thoughts): I'm glad you liked my résumé and invited me to this interview because I'm very interested in pursuing a career with S & O. [With this sentence, Alice has followed

Table 8.1 Alice's "Why You Should Hire Me" (WYSHM) chart.

Attributes Needed	Why I Have What You Need	
	Positive Characteristics	Example
By accounting firms in general:		
Analytical approach	Analytical ability	Analyzed ways to set up Good Buy displays.
Negotiating ability	Flexibility, persuasiveness	Negotiated reduced prices for sorority barbecue.
Presenting skills	Poise, sensitivity	Presented case study on Marketing Plan.
Business sense	Business sense	Accepted losses on returned items to retain good will.
Leadership	Leadership	Led co-workers in setting up Good Buy displays.
Communication skills	Good writing skills	Good grades on essays and term papers.
By Sincere & Olde:		
Research	Thoroughness, open-mindedness	Researched impact of FASB 98 on both small and large firms.
Teamwork	Team player	Unit at Good Buy.

up on my opening comment and seized the opportunity to express interest in the firm. Alice then continued with her response to the main part of my question.]

When I researched the public accounting field, I found that a number of attributes for a good accountant were frequently mentioned. For example, a good accountant should have leadership skills. I demonstrated those skills many times—for example, when I galvanized my co-workers at Good Buy Department Store to get a project completed quickly and without a directive from on-high. Another important skill is communication, and I am strong there, particularly in writing. For example, my professors have noted my clear writing style on essays.

Your S & O recruiting brochure mentioned teamwork as being important to the success of the firm. I was elected captain of our intramural softball team because my teammates recognized that I would work for the good of the team and not just my own ego.

To fine-tune Alice's chart, I gave these suggestions:

- Your examples should come from different areas of your life—
  different jobs, academics, extracurricular activities. Draw your
  examples from *several* jobs, not just Good Buy.
- Your examples should be as meaningful as possible. The initial
  example of negotiating (reduced prices for the sorority barbe-
  cue) did not involve much negotiating. Consider adding or sub-
  stituting other examples.
- Try to construct three examples for each characteristic, in case
  you're asked for more than one. If you have several examples,
  you won't be at a loss if you forget one of them.
- Don't be concerned if your chart doesn't contain every Positive
  Characteristic imaginable. *Nobody* has every Positive Characteristic a firm would want.

Preparing her WYSHM chart helped Alice answer my question by citing
three characteristics that the firm needs and Alice can offer, as proven by
concrete examples. Alice chose these particular characteristics because:

- They addressed the question;
- Alice would like to discuss them more, and, by mentioning them in her
  answer, she is prompting the interviewer to follow up on one or more
  of them in the next question. (This question–answer–question cycle
  will be discussed extensively in Chapter 10.)

Alice's WYSHM chart will help Alice answer *any* question based on the
"Why Should We Hire You?" theme. For example:

- "Alice, please tell me what you gained from your summer or part-time
  jobs."
- "Alice, can you give me an example of your research skills?"
- "How would a classmate describe you in three words, Alice?"

This last question intimidates some students; they think they are being
asked to reveal the most sensitive aspects of their personality. The question
actually fits the first peak perfectly. Pick three of your Positive Characteristics, support each with an example, and you've answered the question.

Feeling confident that her WYSHM chart enabled her to answer the
first-peak question, Alice tackled the complementary question, "Why do
you want to work for us?"

Why Do You Want to Work for Us?

"Well, I need a job," Alice told me with a laugh. "True enough," I said. "But the firm already knows that. You want to *use your time well* at the interview, so there's no point in rehashing an obvious fact." I asked Alice to think about what she wanted in three categories: the job, the firm, and the industry or profession.

These three categories would most affect Alice's professional life. Alice took a pad of paper and prepared the rough chart shown as Table 8.2.

Your chart will reflect you as an individual, and most charts should be amended as you think about and rethink the issue at hand. Alice's chart was a good basis for our next step.

"Alice," I said, "in two weeks you're going to interview with Sincere & Olde, one of the largest public accounting firms in the world. Can you tell me how S & O meets what you want in your employer?" Alice told me she knew S & O was one of the "Big Six," but wasn't sure how to find out more. I told Alice that most students would be in the same situation, but, following The Plowman's Principle (see Chapter 3), we identified the ways in which S & O meets Alice's expectations for an employer.

First, I asked Alice to make a mini-chart by picking one item from each category on her main chart. Alice chose these pairs:

Category	What I Want
The job	Variety
The firm	Good client base
Profession	Opportunity to move into private industry

Next, I asked Alice to read through S & O's *recruiting literature* to determine what the firm told prospective employees. Two days later, Alice came back with the *expanded mini-chart* shown as Table 8.3

"Good work, Alice," I said. "You have identified three things you want that the firm says it offers. That's probably sufficient to answer the 'Why do you want to work for us?' question. Just to make sure, pick another item from each category, make another mini-chart, and repeat the process."

Hector's situation was a bit different from Alice's. Hector was preparing to interview with Manufacturco, a major industrial firm. Its recruiting literature was not as extensive, but its annual report was frequently discussed in the business press. Hector's mix of information sources differed from Alice's, but the *process* for Hector was the same.

A main element in Hector's interview preparation was his use of a list of Fifteen Things to Know About a Company. By using the list as a research

Table 8.2   Alice's "Why I Want to Work for You" (IWW) chart.

Category	What I Want
The job	Variety Challenge Respect Pleasant working environment Good training
The firm	Reputable Well-organized Good client base Professional stature Location
Profession	High ethical standards Opportunity for partnership (including women) Opportunity to move into private industry

Table 8.3   Employer's offerings vs. Alice's goals.

Category	What I Want	What the Firm Offers
The job	Variety	The firm assigns new employees to a variety of audit engagements, typically covering three or four industry groups.
The firm	Good client base	The client base listed in the brochure is diversified and includes many well-known companies.
Profession	Opportunities to move into private industry	The brochure only touches on this, but it indicates that many of its alumni have left the firm for lucrative opportunities, often with S & O clients.

guide and checklist, Hector was able to develop answers for any question similar to: "Tell me what you know about our firm."

FIFTEEN THINGS TO KNOW ABOUT A COMPANY

Research about the firm is one of the critical requirements for succeeding at an interview. *At a minimum,* you should know the information needed to answer the questions below for any publicly held firm (a firm that sells its

When Alice read the S & O literature, she noted that the firm openly discussed the fact that many of its former employees ("alumni") had left to accept positions with other firms, often clients. In the public accounting profession, such openness about the next employer is not unusual. In most other situations, however, the opposite holds true. Your prospective employer will be thinking in terms of your long-term growth within the firm, not where you'll find employment if you choose to leave.

This is the advice I gave Alice:

- Focus on your career potential *within* the firm. Even though the firm openly discusses its "alumni," don't initiate a discussion of prospects beyond the firm at your interview. If your interviewer takes up the subject, it's fine to express awareness of the career potential with other employers.
- Discuss *only* the career you want to build within the firm, or you will seriously harm your chances of getting a job offer. Most firms do not openly discuss your career prospects if you leave them for another employer.

stock to the public). For privately held firms (those that do not sell their stock to the public), information about profits, revenue, and number of employees may not be obtainable.

1. What is the firm's line of business?
2. What are the products it produces or the services it provides? (Be specific.)
3. How large is the firm, in terms of gross revenue and total employees?
4. When was the firm established?
5. What was the firm's profit/loss last year?
6. What has been the trend of the firm's profits over the past few years?
7. How is the firm organized, for example, how many divisions does the firm have? Does the firm seem to be organized along product lines, service functions, or another basis? Why?
8. How did the chairman or CEO describe the firm's performance in the most recent annual report?
9. What major challenges does the firm face over the next few years?
10. What plans does the firm have to meet those challenges?
11. Who are the firm's major competitors and where does this firm rank in size (or market share) with its competitors?

12. In what ways does the firm believe it is a good place to work?
13. Describe the state of the firm's *industry* (changing or static; new technologies; profitability; hopeful signs; danger signs).
14. What external events (the economy, the EEC, war) could impact on this company and in what ways?
15. Describe at least *two* news items about the firm that you found in a newspaper or other periodical.

RESEARCHING A PUBLICLY HELD FIRM

The Annual Report

Hector and I planned his research strategy for Manufacturco, which is a publicly held firm (it is owned by shareholders who can trade their shares in the stock market). We knew that, at a minimum, its *annual report* was publicly available. In addition, Manufacturco published *recruiting literature* designed specifically for college seniors. We also knew that news articles about the firm probably appeared in both the *general press* and *trade publications.* Hector and I decided that he would start his research with the firm's annual report, which was available in Emeritus's library. (If your school library doesn't keep annual reports on reserve, you can call a firm's headquarters to request that an annual report be sent to you.) Hector reviewed the Fifteen Things to Know About a Company to help his note taking as he read the annual report.

Hector knew the value of getting an overview of the contents of something you're about to read. He looked through Manufacturco's latest annual report and noticed that a thumbnail sketch of the firm was on the inside cover, financial highlights were presented on early pages, and detailed data were at the end. In between were: a message to shareholders from the firm's chairman, pictures and descriptions of the firm's products, and plenty of photos showing smiling employees.

Although every firm's annual report will be different in some way, Manufacturco's was not atypical. Let's see how Hector used each part of Manufacturco's report to help him with his research.

The *inside cover* was brief but very helpful. It stated that Manufacturco "is a leader in engines and related parts. Our products and services include large turbines, automotive engines, spare widgets, and general gadgets." That information, in a nutshell, told Hector what line of business the firm is in, the first of the Fifteen Things.

The *financial highlights* page had a chart and several graphs. The first graph showed that Manufacturco's revenue had grown from about $10 million in its initial year of operation (1962) to $430 million in 1991. Hector noticed that the vertical bars showing revenue were constantly higher each year, indicating steady growth. But what were Manufacturco's profits, its revenue minus expenses? Hector found a chart that showed 1991 "income" (profits, in everyday language) of $137 million, an increase of 15 percent over the previous year. From this page, Hector learned about the firm's gross revenue, when it was established, and its profit for the past year (three more of the Fifteen Things). Hector didn't know yet about total employees or about the *trend* in profits.

Hector next read Manufacturco's *chairman's message*. The first sentence announced: "We are pleased to report that 1991 was the 28th consecutive year of increased sales and earnings for Manufacturco." Hector noted that earnings (profits) had been on an upward trend, just like revenue. Because profits don't always move in the same direction as revenue, this was useful information. The chairman discussed some details about stock splits, but Hector realized that this information was probably not critical for his purposes.

The chairman's next paragraph seemed mundane, but Hector paused to think about it. "During the year, Manufacturco successfully passed on the metal price increases of last November. The increase in metal prices we anticipated for April did not materialize and we do not anticipate any further increases this calendar year." Manufacturco used large amounts of metal, and the ability to pass price increases to customers affected the firm's profit. "Is this a challenge the firm is addressing?," Hector asked himself.

The chairman then reviewed capital expenditures (investments) for new plant capacity as the firm completed its third year of a Five-Year Expansion Program. Apparently, Manufacturco was confident that there would be demand for its products. Hector asked himself two questions: "Is there a risk that Manufacturco has *over*expanded? What role do the financial analysts at Manufacturco have in these investment decisions?" These questions were related to Hector's goal of becoming a financial analyst at Manufacturco, and he made note of them as possible questions to ask at his interview.

The chairman continued his message with a review of the past year. "In 1991," he wrote, "the Firm did accomplish our objectives." He then cited the key objectives: cost control, expansion of manufacturing capability, and penetration of new markets. For the forthcoming year, the chairman indicated, Manufacturco's goals were: improving cost controls, maintaining financial strength, opening new markets, and reinvesting in the company. Hector realized two things. First, the goals for the new year were similar to those of the previous year. Second, given the emphasis on cost control, reinvestment, and financial strength, financial analysts would seem to have an important role to play in the firm. The last part of the chairman's message addressed, at least partially, items 8, 9, and 10 of the Fifteen Things (the chairman's view of performance; some challenges to be faced). Hector had identified two areas he might want to ask about at his interview (risk of overexpansion, and role of financial analysts in meeting the firm's objectives).

Hector already had some sense of the firm's line of business, record, and objectives when he turned to the next section in Manufacturco's annual report: *product descriptions*. Manufacturco produced and sold four major products; each product was made by a distinct division of the firm. Hector wrote down the names of the major products:

- Terrific Turbines;
- Mar-vel Motors;
- Wonder Widgets;
- General Gadgets.

For each product, the main clients were listed. Hector noticed that two of the divisions were recent acquisitions. "I wonder if they use a uniform method of financial controls and reporting," Hector, the future financial analyst, asked himself.

Hector proceeded to read through the extensive financial data at the end of Manufacturco's report. He remembered my advice to look for key facts identified by the Fifteen Things and not spend his time with topics like earnings per share and working capital. Realizing that he should spend his research time where it would strengthen his interview most, Hector found a chart on Manufacturco's operations that showed:

- Net income (that is, after-tax profits) had risen consistently from $10 to $36 million over the previous 10 years;
- The number of employees was 2,900.

Hector looked through the rest of the categories in the financial data but found no other information related to the Fifteen Things.

Hector wanted a clear picture of what he knew and didn't know about Manufacturco before he proceeded with his research. Based on the Fifteen Things to Know About a Company, he made the chart shown as Table 8.4.

Hector was glad he had made his research chart. It helped him to organize the notes he had taken about what he had learned so far and to identify quickly the areas where he was still in the dark.

Recruiting Literature

Manufacturco produced a recruiting brochure designed especially for college students, and Hector knew that he should use it to continue his research. At the very least, it would tell Hector what Manufacturco wanted people to think about it.

Table 8.4   Hector's research chart.

Topic	Summary of Information	Source
1. Line of business	Turbines, motors, computer parts	Annual report
2. Products/services	Manufactures turbines, motors, widgets, and gadgets; spare parts and service for its products.	Annual report
* 3. Size	Revenue, $430 million (1991); employees, 2,900	Annual report
4. Established	1962	Annual report
* 5. Net profit, 1991	$36 million	Annual report
* 6. Profit trend	?	?
7. Organization	Four divisions, by product line	Annual report
8. Performance	Met key objectives	Annual report
9. Challenges	Controlling costs; passing along cost increase	Annual report
	Competition	?
	Regulation	?
10. Meet challenges	Cost control program and profit-sharing plan; passalong?	Annual report
11. Competitors: Size comparison	Not identified yet	?
12. Good place to work	Not identified yet	?
13. State of industry	Not identified yet	?
14. External events	Not certain (war, economy, competition, computer technology)	?
15. News items	Need to research	?

Ask about: Uniform financial controls; overexpansion risk; role of financial analysts

*These items will be difficult to answer for a *privately held* firm, like a partnership.

The recruiting brochure was titled "Manufacturco: Our Financial Management Program." "Not an inspiring title," Hector decided. "I just hope it's informative."

The brochure started with a brief description of Manufacturco that was consistent with the annual report, but less extensive. "It's a good thing I didn't rely on this brochure only," thought Hector.

The next section caught Hector's eye: "The Strategic Role of Finance" at Manufacturco. Its first paragraph was:

At Manufacturco, financial managers take a leadership role in major business decisions. They are not just number crunchers. Our financial people have major input into our decisions on acquisitions, cost control, and maintaining financial strength. These areas are critical to Manufacturco's future. In addition, our financial managers play a key role in keeping our four divisions working for the overall good of the firm through the implementation of our internally devised Uniform Financial Controls (UFC).

Hector was glad to read that finance has a major role in Manufacturco, even though it seems to be a manufacturing-driven company. "Now I know that Uniform Financial Controls are in place. I'll make a note of that term. UFC seems to be an in-house buzz word worth remembering.

"OK, I have a sense of what financial *managers* do. What about financial analysts?," Hector wondered. The next section, captioned "Financial Management Program (FMP): What It Offers," addressed Hector's question directly:

At Manufacturco, our FMP is an intensive $2^{1}/_{2}$-year program that combines on-the-job experience with formal classroom training. Our goal is to prepare you for a leadership role in our business. Your training assignments will be "real-world," with responsibility for real decisions. You will move to a new assignment every six months. Our classroom will provide you with challenge and technical skills without making you feel that you're back in college again.

Hector noted that there was an apparent *balance* between classroom training and on-the-job assignments and that the assignments were real and not just practice.

Library Sources

One good source of current information on hundreds of industries is *Standard & Poor's Industry Surveys* (SPIS). When Hector opened the SPIS in the main library's reference room, he noted that the material was cross-referenced in an index containing the names of about 1,000 firms. Hector looked at this list and saw that Manufacturco was mentioned on pages E20 to E22. When Hector turned to those pages, he saw that they were within the survey of "Engines."*

"That's great," Hector thought. "I can find the appropriate industry survey by looking in the *index of companies.*"

---

* I have synthesized this section. In the SPIS, there is no section entitled "Engines."

From the description of the current situation regarding "Engines," Hector noted that the industry was hurt by the slowdown in auto sales, because car manufacturers were major purchasers of engines. Hector also read that Happyco and Dollarco were now challenging Manufacturco's market dominance in widgets and gadgets. In general, the engine industry was counting on expanded markets—at home for autos, and abroad for widgets and gadgets—to absorb the surplus production capacity engines had experienced in 1991. "This industry, in general, is facing economic challenges, and Manufacturco has some new competitors. I wonder what Manufacturco plans to do about this problem," Hector said to himself. He noted on his research chart this new information about challenges and competitors.

To research the business press and the general press, Hector went to the Info Trac section of the reference library. On the Info Trac computer, Hector could find articles about Manufacturco, engines in general, and important customers like the auto industry. Hector wrote down several citations for articles in *The Wall Street Journal* and *The New York Times*. An article in *The Wall Street Journal*, "Slugfest in Engineland: Manufacturco and Rivals in a Dog-Fight," seemed especially relevant. Hector noted that the reference was fairly recent and went to the periodicals section of the library to get the issue he needed. The article told how Happyco and Dollarco were trying to take away Manufacturco's market share and how Manufacturco was fighting back. A chart showed the relative size of each firm and the share of the market it held. "This is great," said Hector. "Now I know something about Manufacturco relative to its competitors. This article also adds some information I didn't get from the SPIS."

When I saw Hector again, I recommended two *very quick* ways to get some extra information:

- Call Manufacturco and ask for the public relations or shareholder relations department. Many firms will be glad to send you a *media kit* containing current news releases about products, profits, and plans.
- Ask a *stockbroker* to send you a copy of his or her firm's recommendations for buying or selling Manufacturco stock. Many brokerage houses will be glad to oblige, at no cost to you. What you'll get is a current, outsider's evaluation of Manufacturco's status and prospects.

If you follow in Alice's and Hector's footsteps:

- You will be able to answer well the twin peaks questions;
- You will be able to answer the frequently asked question: "Please tell me what you know about our company";
- You will show your interviewer that you are truly interested in his or her firm and that you come prepared to meetings;
- You will be more successful with the questions you ask at the end of your interview;
- You will take a major step toward allaying your interview anxiety, because you will know you are well-prepared.

Let's take a look at the second key to your successful interviewing: Axing Anxiety.

CHAPTER NINE

Axing Anxiety

In this chapter, I will tell you how to reduce your interview anxiety. We will listen in on a session of the Job Search Club at which I put the members more at ease by debunking Seven Great Interview Myths.

IS ANYONE NERVOUS?

Typically, I start off a Job Search Club interview preparation session by asking whether anyone is nervous about interviewing. The question is usually followed by widespread nervous laughter and a show of a few hands. Our discussion at a typical session should be helpful to you as you are preparing for an interview.

Richard: Is there anyone who is at least a little bit nervous about interviewing?

David: I'm not sure that I have the right personality for interviewing. How should we act at an interview?

Richard: David, you've just touched on a major myth.

THE MYTH OF THE RIGHT PERSONALITY

There's no such thing as the ideal interview personality.

Whatever personality you have is as ideal as you need. The key is to be *yourself* at *your best.* Enthusiasm, for example, is a very positive personality characteristic, but this does not mean that there is some predetermined Enthusiastic Personality. You can communicate enthusiasm in *many ways* during an interview. However, your enthusiasm will show best if you:

Have done your homework by thoroughly researching the firm;

Ask well-thought-out, focused questions;

Make an effort to "sell" your candidacy to the firm by demonstrating *why* you should be hired.

You will then reflect the *time* and *effort* you have *put in* preparing for your interview, not external behaviors that you *put on* during your interview.

Don't worry that you're not Mr. or Ms. Right and don't try to be someone you're not. *You* exist; Mr. or Ms. Right does not. You *at your best* will succeed at your interview.

Gabrielle: Well, I'm concerned that my mind will just go blank at the interview.

Richard: Remember that it's not very common for a person to go absolutely blank at an interview. But suppose you did. You could simply indicate that the job means so much to you that you're really nervous and aren't sure you have a good understanding of the interviewer's question. Then ask the interviewer to repeat the question. You might say something like this: "This job means a lot to me and I'm very nervous. I'm not sure I understood your question. Would you mind restating it?"

> One of the things to remember is that, at an interview, *everybody* is nervous, including the interviewer. Don't be nervous *about being nervous.* If you feel that nervousness is interfering with your interview, you don't have to hide the feeling. For example, you could say to the interviewer: "You know, [interviewer's name], I'm really nervous. This is one of my first interviews and I really want this job. I hope that my nervousness won't get in the way of our interview." Acknowledging your nervousness may even make you feel more at ease.

Robert: My concern is related to Gabrielle's in a way. I'm concerned that I'll say something foolish.

Richard: Robert, what is the worst thing that could happen if you did say something foolish?

Robert: Two "worst things": I wouldn't get the job, and I would feel foolish among my friends afterward.

I told Robert I was glad he had raised this point because it troubles many students. They go through the interview hoping they won't say anything foolish. Their worrying diverts their energy from their main goal—to move toward a job offer by getting invited to a Site Visit.

Richard: It's unlikely that any one thing you will say is going to destroy your interview. The interviewer evaluates the *entire* interview before making a recommendation about inviting you to the Site Visit (or second interview).

Remember that only two people in the world will know what you say at the interview—you, and the interviewer, who won't care after he or she finishes evaluating you. What you say will not be plastered around your favorite gathering place or published in the campus newspaper.

In the worst case imaginable, you won't get the job—and let's not exaggerate the implications of that outcome. You'll be disappointed but still alive to interview with other firms.

Gabrielle: Richard, I have a more fundamental problem. I don't have any relevant experience.

I told Gabrielle that she had just identified the No Relevant Experience Myth. Like most people, you have not done *during* college the kind of work you want to do *after* college. In fact, you probably couldn't, because a college degree would have been required.

THE NO RELEVANT EXPERIENCE MYTH

Remember that the interviewer, like the original résumé reader, is trying to *predict*, based on your past and present, whether you would make a good future employee. The difference is that the résumé reader had only a piece of paper to work from. The interviewer has you in person.

Your goal, then, is to bring out those characteristics that would be useful to your prospective employer. We have seen that the key to using your work experience is identifying your Positive Characteristics—for example, what you have *demonstrated, achieved, and learned* in part-time and summer jobs (of whatever kind) and extracurricular activities. If you can show those characteristics, it is *secondary* whether you gained them at a typical survival job or at IBM. In brief,

- Show what you can bring to your *next* job;
- Remember that the significant thing about your *past* is what it *predicts* about your future.

I told Gabrielle about Terri, who had been a marketing senior a year earlier.

THE ONLY THE ALL-STARS CAN PLAY MYTH

Terri was in some distress when she came to see me. She was getting ready for an interview and was stuck on an exercise I had given her—namely, to cite three examples of her persuasive ability and three examples of her leadership. "I've never sold anybody anything and I've never been a club officer," Terri said. "What can I say about persuasion and leadership?"

Terri could have helped herself by viewing the situation this way: "Let me think of examples of my persuasive ability and leadership. I know that a good source of things to look at is what I've been doing on my part-time and summer jobs, in the dormitory, and as a club member. Let me make some lists." Looked at this way, the question doesn't require any particular work experience or elective office, and that's the point I wanted to make for Terri.

I asked Terri about her student aide job in the admissions office. "Nothing spectacular" she said. I agreed, but "spectacular" isn't the issue. I narrated my dialogue with Terri to the JSC group.

Richard: Describe a day in the admissions office.
Terri: Well, people come to me and ask questions about the school. Sometimes they're a little hostile and ask about campus security and the impact of the budget cuts.
Richard: What do you do then?
Terri: I tell them that I've been here for three years and feel very safe. In terms of the budget cuts, they've caused some problems, but I've still been able to get every course I needed.
Richard: How do the potential new students react?
Terri: They generally seem to feel more comfortable with our school. I know that because they start to ask me the kind of questions you ask when you're seriously considering attending a certain school.
Richard: Did you persuade them to be more open-minded about the school?
Terri (with a smile):   Yes; I guess that's an example of persuasion, isn't it?

The lesson Terri learned was that *you don't have to be an all-star* to have demonstrated important skills and abilities. In many cases, what you've done in *common situations* will favorably impress an interviewer. But it's your job to *identify* the *examples.*

Hector then asked me a classic student question:

Hector: Richard, you've been telling us to go into the interview wanting the job offer. But I don't want to be dishonest—I don't know what I really want.
Richard: Hector, I admire your honesty, but it would be more constructive for you to view the issue in its proper context. The issue, properly understood, *is not* "This is the *one* and *only* job I want." You only need to feel that this is *a* job in which you have some serious interest. You might want *many* jobs before you find one that is offered to you and accepted by you.

Many students find this suggestion helpful: At an interview, focus your answer on what *attracts you to that job*. This does not preclude you from being attracted to other jobs as well. Presented that way, you are being honest with yourself and the interviewer. Honesty is not monogamy at the interview stage.

To put interviewing in a social context, your interview is more like having a first date than suggesting to someone that it's time to get married. You are saying "I think you're cute," not "I love you."

Alice raised her hand and asked, "How will I know if I've answered the interviewer's question?"

I told Alice that this might seem like a prodigious problem, but it really isn't.

Richard: Your answer should be *brief*—say, five or six sentences. Long answers lose impact, get off the subject, and bore the listener. If you have any doubt that you've answered the question, *ask the interviewer* rather than sitting there with the doubt. You could say, simply, "Have I answered your question?" or "Would you like me to tell you more?"

Robert, an anthropology major, said he wanted to ask a related question.

Robert: Very often, I don't know *how I want to answer a question*. It's embarrassing to sit there going "umm."

Richard: Robert, that's a good point. Now imagine that you're at a business meeting and someone asks you a question. Would you just jump in with an answer or would you pause a moment to reflect?

Robert (pausing):   I think I would pause for a moment. No one expects you to react like a real-time computer at a business meeting. A businessperson should reflect a moment to think, so the response will be concise and meaningful.

Richard: Exactly; remember that a job interview is like a *business meeting between equals*. Pause for a moment to collect your thoughts. You might say something like: "That's a good question. I'd like to think about it for a moment." Identify for yourself a few points you want to make, and then proceed with your answer. A pause will make your answer better organized and more forceful. It will *not* make you seem dim-witted or uncertain of yourself.

Alice said she had a related concern. "I'm worried that I won't say what they want to hear." I thanked Alice for introducing The Duck on the Ceiling Myth, which plagues too many students.

THE DUCK ON THE CEILING MYTH

When you enter your interview room, look up to see whether there's a duck on the ceiling. Let me tell you why. Some years ago, Groucho Marx, one of the greatest comedians of the twentieth century, hosted a quiz show called "You Bet Your Life." Before the quizzing began, Groucho would give the contestants a brief interview about their jobs, where they came from, their families, their hobbies, and other topics from their personal lives. The contestants knew that Groucho had picked some common vocabulary word— let's say "kitchen"—and designated it as the special word of the evening. The audience knew the special word, but the contestants did not. Groucho attached the word to a *stuffed duck* that was hoisted to the ceiling at the beginning of the show. If a contestant said the "right" word, the duck came down from the ceiling and the contestant won a few hundred dollars. The audience had a great time watching for the contestants to say the "right word." The duck usually stayed on the ceiling.

Groucho's show was hilarious and had a nationwide audience of loyal fans. *But there is no duck hanging from the ceiling at a job interview!* There is no predetermined right (or wrong) answer that the interviewer is expecting to hear. The interviewer *wants to hear what you have to say* and will evaluate your response on its own merits.

There are two additional reasons for not expending mental energy in trying to guess what the interviewer wants to hear.

- If you *try* to read the interviewer's mind, you will undercut a key aspect of your mental preparation—the sense that an interview is a *business meeting between equals*. Don't turn the interview into a half-hour of *guessing* what someone else wants to hear; *know what you want to say* about yourself that would make you a good employee.
- You will jeopardize the interviewer's confidence that you are giving honest answers if you try to anticipate what he or she wants to hear. Honest answers come from your own feelings and experiences, not from what you imagine is in someone else's head.

The Creation Epic: An Interviewing Perspective

In the beginning, the Creator considered how best to fashion humans. There were many things to take into account—muscles, circulation, growth potential, spiritual development. The Creator also determined that humans' very structure would be a lesson in how to do things right. Therefore, the Creator determined that humans should have:

Two ears: to emphasize the importance of listening;

A brain: placed deliberately between the ears to help humans think about what others were heard to say;

A mouth: for speaking, but only after hearing and thinking first.

The Creator looked upon humans and saw that they were good, especially for interviewing.
And thus it is that

Listen

Think

Respond

became an interviewing creed for all time.

David asked about a subject that troubles students far more than it's worth. "What about dress? I read that 'Dress makes the person,' but I don't have a lot of money. What do you suggest?"

I told David that he could learn to *dress without distress.*

THE DRESS IS CRITICAL MYTH

If you are a man, wear a suit (dark is best, light is OK), a shirt (solid blue or white makes it easier to match your outfit), a tie, socks, and shoes. You don't need to find out what the Power Tie of the Year is. Just have a clean tie that matches your shirt and suit. If you are a woman, wear a skirt and blouse or a woman's suit. Be modest—you're going to a business meeting, not a dinner date. *These simple rules are sufficient.* As a placement director, I have sponsored 25,000 interviews, and *not once* has a student who followed these simple guidelines hurt his or her chances at an interview. Once, an interviewer remarked that the way a candidate dressed *helped* her get a second interview.

You cannot score points by the way you dress. If you dress as I have just indicated, you will *neutralize the issue,* which is the most you can hope for anyway.

When you are actually in a profession, certain standards may apply. After you join a particular firm, your wardrobe may change. Until then, be neat, clean, and professional. Anything more is not necessary.

Hitches and Glitches

Don't destroy your chances by *looking unprofessional.* Blue jeans, casual slacks, and sneakers are out; so is scuba-diving equipment or attention-grabbing attire. If your dress is casual, Modern Day Student style, the interviewer can assume either that you are not serious about the job or that your elevator doesn't go to the top floor. Be serious or be unemployed.

THE LEARNER'S PERMIT MYTH

Bill asked me a good question that helped clarify his purpose at the interview—to move toward a job offer by getting invited to a Site Visit.

Bill: If the firm is learning about us at the interview, shouldn't we be learning about the firm as well?

Richard: That's a good question, Bill. You may learn something about the firm at your interview, but that's not your objective. Your objective at your interview is to progress toward a job offer. All your energy should be directed to that goal.

There are four good reasons why trying to learn about the job should *not be your goal* at your interview:

1. You should have learned about the firm through your research *before* your interview, as a basic part of your preparation. If your interest is to learn about the firm during your interview, you are liable to be less thorough in your research about the firm *beforehand.* That approach could be fatal to your chances.
2. If you make learning about the firm an interview goal, you will tend to evaluate the job while you are still in the interview. The job hasn't been offered yet, so an evaluation at this point would be meaningless. Besides, if you try to evaluate the job under the stress of an interview, you won't be able to make a sound judgment anyway.

3.   You should be selling your Positive Characteristics, not trying to learn, at an interview. Learning tends to be a reflective, almost passive, activity for many people. That attitude will usually work against you at an interview. You should be proactive and enthusiastic, to get the job offer.
4.   You can ask anything you want about the job or the firm *after* the offer is in your hand. At that point, you can ask questions and evaluate the job in a calm and thoughtful manner.

Does that mean that you shouldn't learn about the firm at the interview? No! But learning is not your goal. What you want to do is listen carefully to what your interviewer says and use it to help you *move toward the job offer.*

Alice, an accounting major, objected to something I had said. "How can you tell us that an interview is like a business meeting between equals? Isn't the employer in the driver's seat?"

I told Alice that her question was important for debunking the Ten-Foot-Tall-Interviewer Myth.

THE TEN-FOOT-TALL INTERVIEWER MYTH

Larry, who was not a JSC member, came to my office one Monday in a state of agitation. His first interview was scheduled for the next day. I asked him how he felt. "It's unfair," Larry told me. I wondered what was unfair; had I done something wrong?

"No, that's not it. I've worked so hard for 3½ years, in part because I wanted a good job. Tomorrow, I have 30 minutes to make the guy from Toolco happy. He could ruin my life by giving me a thumbs-down.

I told Larry I thought he was exaggerating the importance of one interview for his whole life, but, more to the point, I still wasn't sure exactly what was "unfair."

"Look," Larry explained, with his hand stretched two feet over his head, "this corporate guy can look at me and decide whether I get a job." As Larry said "me," his hand indicated a height below his knees.

Now I had the picture: the Student Pygmy against the Corporate Giant. I gave Larry two pieces of advice:

- Get the situation straight. An interview is not even a contest, let alone a joust to the death. It's a business meeting.
- There are no pygmies or giants at your meeting. There are only actively involved people participating as equals.

Larry was still a little unconvinced, so I suggested a teeth-brushing fantasy. If your interviewer seems like a ten-foot-tall corporate giant, imagine his or her going through daily teeth-brushing rituals, or any other activity we all do every day. Such an image usually cuts your image of the interviewer down to realistic size.

The interview is being held because both you as a job seeker and the firm as an employer want to see whether there is a good match between you. If there is, the firm may offer to give you a salary in exchange for your labor. This is a business meeting about a business deal. If the firm makes you an offer, you may accept it—*or reject it!*

In this chapter, you have learned to allay your interviewing anxiety by debunking the seven great interview myths.

If you feel less anxious now, let the business meeting between equals begin.

CHAPTER TEN

The Business Meeting Between Equals

In this chapter, I will show you how to promote your Positive Characteristics at your interview, how to set at least part of the interview agenda by your answer to the first question, and how to make use of the question–answer–question cycle. You will learn why examples are critical to your success and how you should construct them. Finally, I will give you my suggested approach to answering 20 different interview questions and will tell you how to use your résumé as a source of practice interview questions. We will also discuss the ethics of honesty at your interview.

This chapter and the two that follow will look at the structure of your interview, section by section, and see how you can succeed by promoting your Positive Characteristics. The basics of your initial interview with a firm are the same whether the interview is held on-campus or in the firm's offices.

The five typical phases of an interview, and their approximate lengths, are:

1. Small talk (ice breaker)—a few minutes;
2. Opening question—a few minutes;
3. Follow-up questions—15 to 20 minutes;
4. *Your* questions—about 5 minutes (discussed in Chapter 11);
5. Closing: Ask for the Job—1 or 2 minutes (discussed in Chapter 12).

Generally, an initial interview takes about 30 minutes.

SMALL TALK

Your interview is likely to begin with a low-keyed question—"Can you believe this weather?" or "Have you been following the college football team?" This kind of question has three purposes.

- The interviewer wants to break the ice with you. The best way is to ask something you won't find threatening.
- The interviewer wants to put you at ease. If you are less nervous, the interview will be more informative—a benefit to both you and the interviewer.
- A low-keyed question helps the interviewer to see whether you can make small talk—a useful skill in business. In some firms, if you can't make small talk, you won't get the job.

The small-talk period *is not wasted time.* It's an opportunity for you to become comfortable with the interview room environment and to practice listening to what your interviewer has to say. In that sense, it's like the time given to a pitcher to warm up before the start of a game. Even though the warm-up pitches don't count on the official record, the warm-up is essential to success in the game.

OPENING QUESTION

After a few minutes of small talk, your interviewer will ask the first question that is related to the heart of your interview. Typical opening questions might be:

- "Alice, tell me why you chose to attend Emeritus College."
- "Bill, why did you decide to become a marketing major?"
- "Craig, please tell me about yourself."

Your answer to this first question is especially important because:

- The interviewer is likely to ask one or two *follow-up* questions based on your answer. If you include in your response the topics *you would like to discuss further,* you can set the agenda for your interview, at least partially.
- During the first five minutes, the interviewer usually forms an impression of you, whether positive or negative; the rest of the interview serves to confirm that initial impression. The interviewer will tend to hear what supports his or her initial impression and to screen out information that conflicts with it.

A typical opening question was handled nicely by Alice in an interview early in her senior year. Alice was an accounting major who was interested in starting a career in public accounting. She had good grades (GPA 3.6), but she knew that grades alone wouldn't get her through the interview process. Based on her informational interviews, Alice considered the characteristics that would be appealing to a public accounting firm and determined that she was strong in four areas: academic excellence, self-reliance, communication, and leadership. In preparing to bring out those qualities in her interviews, she outlined for herself how she could introduce those points in response to an opening question. This was the opening-question dialogue.

Interviewer: Alice, tell me why you chose to attend Emeritus College.
Alice: I chose to attend Emeritus College because it has a good academic reputation, you can select some very interesting courses, and I could afford the tuition. I knew that I would be paying for a good portion of my expenses, so this was an important consideration.

I am glad I came to Emeritus. In addition to a good education, which challenged me to think, I learned how to be self-reliant, a good communicator, and a leader among my peers.

FOLLOW-UP QUESTIONS

To a clear, concise answer like Alice's, an interviewer will likely follow up by asking more about one of the topics mentioned in the answer. Alice had introduced four topics: academic excellence, self-reliance, communication, and leadership.

Interviewer: Alice, you mentioned that you are a leader among your peers. Can you tell me how you have developed your leadership skills.
*Alice (listens for the **intent** of the question:* to initiate discussion of *examples* of her leadership; decides to give three examples of the leadership she has shown while in college):   My first leadership position at the University was as a residence hall delegate. I organized students on my floor to demand that loud music be banned after 10:00 P.M. during the week. The next year, I was elected president of the business club. I chaired meetings, delegated tasks to members, and represented the club in front of the student council.

I'll give you another example. Last summer, I worked as an intern at Good Buy Department Stores. We were breaking down several old displays when word came that the chairman was going to visit our floor. Even though I had no formal authority, I persuaded the other workers to skip lunch so that we could finish breaking down the old displays and put up the new ones before 1:00 P.M. Was that chairman impressed by the ideas in our new displays! It's a good thing we got them up so fast.

The interviewer may wish to follow up on one of Alice's examples. The interviewer's goals would be to see whether Alice can discuss a subject in more depth and whether Alice's story is credible.

How Should You Address Your Interviewer?

- Your interview is a business meeting between equals. If the interviewer calls you by your first name, it is not rude to use first-name address in reply.
- You should feel comfortable with the address you use. If a first name feels awkward, use "Mr." or "Ms."
- You are usually safer being conservative. If rubbing your interviewer the wrong way is a major concern, use "Mr." or "Ms."

Interviewer: Alice, that was an interesting story about Good Buy Department Stores. Why do you think the other workers listened to you, even at the cost of skipping lunch. Surely it wasn't in their job description.

Alice paused a moment here, to collect her thoughts. She thought about the point of the question: Alice's role in the situation. What was it about Alice's reasoning, presentation, or relationship with her co-workers that persuaded them to skip lunch and set up the displays? Alice responded in terms of *her role* in the situation.

Alice: That's a good question. Let me think about it for a minute. (Pauses a moment to collect her thoughts.) I think there were several reasons why my co-workers listened to me. First, I had a good point to make. We all wanted to be known as the best department in the store. What better way than impressing the chairman? Second, I said it in the right way— not like an order, but more like a challenge. Besides, over the course of the summer, we were becoming friends. When the other workers saw how important it was to me to get the displays up, they decided to pitch in. After we all agreed to skip lunch, I announced that I was buying pizza and soda for the whole crew after work. A happy chairman and a delicious pizza—not bad!

Alice showed that she can discuss a subject in greater depth and she identified three important characteristics (good reasoning, appropriate communication style, and friendship building). In addition, she made her opening response believable by backing it up—and added a spontaneous note of light humor to boot! The interviewer went on to another subject from Alice's opening response.

The Question–Answer–Question Cycle

This brief excerpt from Alice's interview is an example of the question–answer-question cycle. When you understand how the cycle works, use it to your advantage, just as Alice did.
Let's review what happened.

- The interviewer asked Alice why she had chosen to attend Emeritus College.
- Alice listened to the question and directed her response to it.
- Alice included in her response the qualities she wanted followed. Based on her preparation, Alice knew that those qualities were important to the interviewer's firm and that she was strong in those areas.
- The interviewer followed up on leadership because Alice had raised interesting and relevant points that were worth more interview time, and because the follow-up gave the interview an easy flow rather than having a constant stop-and-start pattern.
- Alice addressed the second question with examples that validated her claim to have leadership characteristics.
- The interviewer followed up on one of those examples with a third question, directed toward Alice's work experience. (Some interviewers might have chosen an academic example.) In asking *how* Alice had managed to succeed as a leader, the real questions were: Was Alice's claim to leadership credible and could she discuss a subject in some depth?
- When Alice addressed the third question, she gave plausible reasons for her being a successful leader, and each of her reasons represented a positive characteristic. Alice thus prompted the interviewer to ask a question based on these additional Positive Characteristics.
- The interviewer decided to refer in the fourth question to Alice's first answer, *not* her third answer. The question–answer-question cycle was restarted, and Alice had set the possible topics for this new cycle by what she had included in her answer to the first question.

Interviewer: I'm really impressed about your leadership, Alice. I wonder if you could tell me how you managed to finance so much of your education while you were so involved with your extracurricular activities and your academics.

Alice then had a chance to discuss not only her *self-reliance* but also her *time-management skills.* She was able to set the agenda, at least for the early part of her interview. You can set the agenda, too. The strategy remains the same, even though every individual is different. *Listen* to the question; *think* about it for a moment; then *respond.* Include the Positive Characteristics you want the interviewer to know about and follow up on.

Let's take another example. Bill, a marketing major, is interviewing today with General Thrills, a firm that makes breakfast cereals. This is how Bill might respond to his opening question.

Interviewer: Bill, why did you decide to become a marketing major?
Bill: One of my main reasons for going to college was to come out with a job. My family isn't rich, and I knew that I would have to work for a living. Marketing graduates seemed to do well professionally.

There's something more. I was curious to learn about how businesses work and how things get done. I have a better understanding now of how my breakfast cereal got all the way from an Iowa cornfield to my local supermarket. My classroom experiences as a marketing major have been even better than I expected.

Bill's brief answer shows that his pragmatic reasons for choosing his major were reinforced by a related intellectual curiosity. These are two of Bill's Positive Characteristics. The interviewer is likely to follow up by asking Bill something specific about his major, what career plans he has developed, or what he has liked best about college. These are three areas Bill has prepared for and wants to discuss.

Craig, a psychology major who is not a JSC member, wants to build a career in bank operations. When he was asked "Please tell me about yourself," instead of giving a historical narrative, Craig felt more comfortable describing himself with adjectives. He chose descriptives that identified his *Positive Characteristics,* especially those that were important for success in bank operations.

Craig: (after pausing to collect his thoughts): I'm a well-organized, hardworking person with good communication and interpersonal skills. I'm the kind of person who really focuses my energy on achieving a goal, once I've identified it. I can give you some examples if you like. [The interviewer will almost surely follow up on one or more of the terms Craig has used to describe himself.]

Interviewer: Craig, you've mentioned some interesting things about yourself. Can you give me an example of your interpersonal skills?

Craig: Let me give you an example from last summer. I was working for a medium-size wholesale hardware distributor. Since my job was to expedite the shipment of orders, I had to communicate with the warehouse workers about which orders had priority and the importance of coordinating schedules with the trucks coming into the loading docks. The president and marketing vice president were especially concerned that orders be sent promptly and correctly, an area where they had had some problems in the past. I had to communicate the goals of the manager to the warehouse workers in a way they could accept. Remember, I was the new kid on the block, and summer help to boot! I also had to let the senior managers know in a nice way that they had to be careful about how much to expect from the warehouse workers or they might feed a growing sense of resentment.

In these few sentences, Craig has:

- Validated his claim to have good communication and interpersonal skills by giving a credible example;
- Demonstrated that he was more than "just a student" by choosing an example from his work life rather than his academic life.
- Showed a sensitivity to reactions to a new employee by his reference to being the "new kid on the block";
- Indicated that he was able to deal with both blue-collar workers and white-collar managers—a critical skill in bank operations management.

WHAT HAPPENS NEXT?

Your interviewer knows that he or she has less than 30 minutes to conduct your interview. The small talk, the initial question, your response, and the resulting follow-up questions will probably take 8 to 10 minutes. Your interviewer can then proceed in three basic ways:

1. *Follow the flow of the discussion in progress.* This approach makes a lot of sense, especially if you have been raising useful points in your answers. For example, your interviewer may follow up by asking you how you managed to work, be involved in extracurricular activities, and still do well academically. You would probably want to respond with a discussion of your time-management skills.

2. *Clarify* or *examine* the items on your résumé. Let's assume, for example, that you have had a part-time job as a table server in a restaurant—not a spectacular job, but you have made the most of it on your résumé:

> Developed ability to retain cheerful exterior even when serving difficult clients. Increased restaurant revenue by persuading customers to order appetizers and drinks. Supervised three other waitpersons on late-evening shift. Worked 20 hours a week during academic periods and 40 hours during vacations.

Giving Examples with Your Answers

Examples give your answers a context and, if they make sense, a good measure of credibility.

Interviewer: Why do you feel you would make a good salesperson?

Your reply (sample):   A good salesperson needs to have several skills that I know I possess. For example, I demonstrated my time-management skills by maintaining good grades while working 15 to 20 hours a week. In the course of my club activities, I utilized my abilities in persuasion. I convinced club members to adopt my programs and ideas despite their initial objections. When I was a receptionist for Happy Corporation, I learned to listen well to what people *really* meant or wanted when they came to my desk.

This type of answer shows that you know some of the *attributes* you would need as a salesperson and you have demonstrated them. You project competence even though you have had no direct selling experience.

Interviewer: What was your greatest achievement while attending college?

Your reply (sample):   Just being admitted was an achievement, because my college is so selective. But the main thing for me is how much I have grown as a person. For example, when I came here, I was fairly narrow in my view of the world. Now, through meeting people from other towns and other countries, I have learned that different people will have different, intelligent viewpoints. I have also learned how to get along comfortably with people from a wide variety of backgrounds.

The interviewer may wish to clarify how you persuaded customers to order more than they had planned; whether showing a cheerful exterior in adverse circumstances made you feel dishonest; or what motivated you to work so hard. Be ready for any of those questions. You might even write your résumé so that it *prompts* those questions.

3. Ask his or her standard questions, following company policy or personal preference. It is impossible to know exactly what a particular interviewer's questions will be, but the sample questions given later in this chapter will prepare you for almost anything that might be asked.

No matter which of the three approaches your interviewer takes, you will be ready to answer well *if* you remember to give examples with your answers and you take the advice in the annotations to the interview questions in this chapter.

TEN COMMON INTERVIEW QUESTIONS

Keep the following principles in mind when you form your response to an interview question:

- Be sure that your answer conveys one or more of your Positive Characteristics.
- Be sure each example you cite is significant. Your choice of major or your summer jobs might be significant; your choice of running shoes is not.
- Avoid the *very* personal when discussing yourself. For example, a discussion of your decisions regarding a romantic relationship is inappropriate. Your interview is a *business meeting.*

1. Why Did You Choose to Attend This College and to Pursue Your Particular Major?

The key here is to show how you make decisions and what motivates you. This was Gabrielle's answer.

Gabrielle: When I started to apply to colleges, there were several things I knew I wanted: a good education, a reasonable tuition, and the chance for an active extracurricular and social life.

I visited several colleges, but Emeritus was most appealing to me because it met the basic criteria I mentioned. I entered without knowing what major to choose. Through friends, I discovered that business courses were interesting and that the business majors at Emeritus seemed to do well professionally. Based on those two factors, I decided to become a business major.

In this response, Gabrielle utilized the principles you should keep in mind. She conveyed at least one Positive Characteristic (she cited careful preparation, and well-balanced goals of education, career, and social life), she supported her statement with a significant example (her process in choosing Emeritus College), and she avoided the *very* personal even though she was discussing an important personal decision.

2. What Were Your Most Favorite Course and Your Least Favorite Course?

Think about the intent of this question. Does it really ask you to rank-order your courses? No. Answer in terms of a course you enjoyed (or didn't enjoy) and indicate why. Alice's response showed that a "favorite" course didn't have to come from business.

Alice: One course I liked a lot was American history. The professor really challenged us to think about the complexity of issues that seemed so simple when we studied them in high school. We had to write a lot of research papers, but the professor took the time to read them and make suggestions, so it was worth the effort.

Alice really did enjoy her American history course, so this is an honest answer. In addition, Alice has let her interviewer know that she possesses intellectual curiosity and interests beyond her major. Those are two Positive Characteristics.

3. What Interests You About a Career in the Field You Are Applying For?

This is a way to probe one of the twin peaks: "Why do you want to work for us?" David, who is interested in a sales career, gave an honest and effective response.

David: I want sales as a career because I know I can succeed and make a very good living. It takes good time management, persuasive skills, and a healthy competitive spirit to succeed at sales, and I have all three. For example, I've been able to earn good grades while working part-time and participating in intramural sports. In softball, I'm the guy who dives head-first to catch a sinking liner if that's what it takes to win. And I'm persuasive. Last semester, for example, I convinced the Student Government to increase its allocation for intramurals even after it had announced a general freeze on everybody's budget.

David has shown that he is motivated by a factor well-understood in sales—money. He has also given examples to show that he has the basic characteristics needed to succeed in the sales profession.

4. What Have You Gained from Your Summer Work Experiences? Compare and Contrast Two of Those Experiences.

This is a two-part question, so pause and think about the two parts of your answer. Then respond to each part separately.

The first part, what you have gained from your summer work experiences, is really a subdivision of a twin peaks question: "Why should we hire you?" This composite answer can be used as a model.

Your reply: I've learned a lot of things from my summer experiences. Let me tell you about a few of them. One thing I learned was how to remain cheerful, at least on the outside, even while in a tense situation. I did this by not taking the situation at hand personally. For example, when I worked at my first summer job, I learned to understand that the client was hassling me as The Employee, not me as a person. That approach put sticky situations in a more bearable perspective.

   When I was a lifeguard at Hampton Beach, I learned how to remain alert to my task—water safety—even when nothing dangerous seemed to be going on. That's important, because if you're not alert, someone can drown in a flash.

Pause before you compare your summer jobs. It is most logical to compare the two jobs you've just mentioned.

Your reply: You asked me to compare and contrast my summer jobs. I'll focus on the two I just mentioned. Both jobs required interaction with the public in ways I couldn't predict, but I had to respond professionally. My first job was very structured; being a lifeguard required more independent judgment.

If you're wondering whether you have answered the interviewer's question, act as you would at a business meeting: clarify the situation.

Your reply: I wonder, have I answered both parts of your question?

The interviewer will probably say "Yes." If, instead, the response is "Please give me some more examples of what you learned from your summer jobs," you will know exactly where to pick up with your response.

5. What Do You See as the Greatest Challenge to our Industry over the Next Five Years?

This may sound like an awesome question, but don't be overwhelmed by it. *You prepared for this question* when you researched the Fifteen Things to Know About a Company.

This was Hector's reply.

Hector: It seems to me that the internationalization of the economy is an enormous challenge. On the one hand, it presents the opportunity to find least-cost suppliers anywhere on the globe and to sell to an enormous market. On the other hand, competitors within the industry can use the same opportunities to reduce *their* costs and expand *their* customer base. That means that this firm will have more factors to take into account when planning its strategy.

Would you like me to tell you where I think other challenges are going to come from?

Interviewer: Yes, I would; I'm very interested in what you've been saying.

Hector: Well, let me say a few things about the role of governments in business. Because of concerns about the environment, public safety, and other issues, our government seems to be getting more involved in areas that would affect the firm, like pollution caused by factories. As the business becomes more international, it will have to deal with many governments, not just one. That could really make things interesting.

6. What Character from History or Literature Do You Admire Most? Why?

This is a straightforward question. The interviewer is probing your interests in history, literature and public affairs (all pluses) and your ability to discuss intelligently a subject of general interest.

Pick *a* character you admire from literature or history (not necessarily the one you admire *most*) or a character from business. After you identify the individual, give a little background, unless it's someone famous like Abraham Lincoln. Then explain what you admire about that person.

If the question refers specifically to a character in business, pick a business personality you studied about in class or can discuss intelligently based on your reading of the business press.

David answered the question this way.

David: One character from history I admire a great deal is Benjamin Franklin. He was one of the greatest people of his generation, excelling in science, business, and literature. Franklin managed to combine high intellect with good humor, and private success with public service. I admire those characteristics.

7. What Was the Most Difficult Decision You Ever Had to Make? How Did You Make That Decision?

Identify *a* difficult decision, not necessarily the most difficult decision you ever had to make.

Every person makes many decisions during life, so your answer has to be your own. Judith, who was not a JSC member but had a particularly strong résumé, gave this response.

Judith (after pausing for a moment to collect her thoughts):   The decision to take a co-op at IBM was very difficult for me. I was just a sophomore, and I really wanted to work as a lifeguard so I could be with my friends. Also, if I lived at home, I could save my salary, but I had to pay my expenses when I went to IBM at Oswego.

On the other hand, I knew that the experience at IBM would be very helpful to my career and that I'd have to learn to live on my own sometime.

I'm glad I made the decision I did. In terms of my career, the IBM co-op gave me a chance to apply my analytical skills in a real corporate context. I also gained confidence by adjusting to a new social environment in a strange place and being happy there.

Judith achieved several objectives with her answer:

- She conveyed some of her Positive Characteristics—a career focus early in college; social maturity; willingness to try something inconvenient and disconcerting as part of a growth experience.
- She made it clear that she was ready to relocate, an important consideration for the company with which she was interviewing that day.
- She strengthened the perception that she could apply her academic skills in a corporate context.

Notice that her response followed the principles I suggested you should keep in mind:

- Convey some Positive Characteristics;
- Choose a significant example;
- Social concerns are o.k., but avoid the *very* personal.

8. Looking Back over Your Years in College, What Do You Wish You Had Learned That You Didn't Learn?

When you look back on your college career, you may find that there are subjects you now wish you had studied. Time constraints or the pressure of required courses may have precluded them. Perhaps only retrospectively are you attracted to academic courses you didn't pursue. If this is the case, feel free to say so. (The course in question need not be in your major.) Be prepared for a follow-up question such as "Why *didn't* you study X?" *Don't apologize;* just explain the reason. Very few people accomplish everything they want to in a limited period of time.

Unless the question specifies *academic* learning, you could discuss cultural or social learning opportunities that you are sorry to have missed.

This is how Alice answered the "looking back" question.

Alice: I have enjoyed my 3½ years at Emeritus College and I am happy with the way I've grown here. Still, as I look back, I wish that I had taken some more courses in history. I think it's important to understand the background of how we got where we are.

I've joined an inexpensive book-of-the-month club that specializes in history. There *is* life after college.

> Life doesn't end with graduation. Educational, social, and cultural opportunities are almost always present in some form everywhere. Indicate how you plan to learn in the future those things you feel you missed in the past. In my own case, I wish I had studied Spanish in college, but I didn't. However, I did study Spanish for two years after I became a placement director. It's never too late.

9. How Would a Friend Describe You in Three Words?

When Bill was asked this question, he kept my principles in mind. I have identified them in Bill's answer. Bill paused for a moment to collect his thoughts before answering. He realized that this question is really like "Why Should We Hire You?" and he mentally reviewed his twin peaks of interviewing chart.

Bill: I think a friend would describe me as hard-working, reliable, and competitive. [Bill is conveying some of his Positive Characteristics.] Let me tell you why. [Bill is about to support his statement with significant examples.]

People notice that I put myself into whatever I do, whether in class or at work. That's why people want to be on class projects with me and why my boss gives me so much responsibility at work. I'm reliable because I'll do whatever is necessary to fulfill a commitment. Last week, I promised to pick up a friend at the train station. My car broke down, but I borrowed a car from another friend and got to the station on time.

Although I like to cooperate with my team, I like to beat the competition, as we did last week in our marketing project. [Bill has avoided comments that are *very* personal.]

10. Are There Any Questions You Would Like to Ask Me?

There had better be! Check out Hector's, in Chapter 11.

What the Questions Represent

These ten questions match the flow of a typical interview. As you think about your possible answers, remember to *give examples* with your answers.

A Résumé–Interview Question Link

Although the primary purpose of your résumé is to get you into the interview room, your résumé may also be used as a source for interview questions. There are several reasons for this link:

- By connecting a question to your résumé, the interviewer may make the question seem more tailored to you as an individual;
- The interviewer may have found something on your résumé that is especially interesting or needs clarification;
- Questions about some of your work experiences may give some insight about how you handle yourself in a job. This is particularly true if the work experience on your résumé is closely related, by function or industry, to the job you are seeking.

Very often, questions drawn from your résumé will be framed as "How" or "Why." A good way to prepare for your interview is to have a friend (or better yet, a stranger) ask you "How," "Why," and "Give me an example" questions as he or she goes down your résumé.

This preparation will help you even if your interviewer doesn't ask you anything directly from your résumé.

These questions are only a sample of what you may hear at an interview. Every interview runs its own course. However, if you practice the questions I have given you and understand the question–answer–question cycle, you will have a solid basis for answering any question at your interview.

A SAMPLING OF DIFFICULT QUESTIONS

Students, over the past years, have shared with me questions they found particularly difficult. Generally, there are no "right" answers to interview questions. However, the questions and sample responses below should be of assistance to you.

1. What Was the Most Difficult Task You Encountered on a Job?

Whenever you are asked for the "most," "best," "worst," or other superlative, remember this: Just think of *an* example, not necessarily the ultimate experience. Here, think of *a* difficult task. Describe the problem and how you overcame it. If possible, tell the interviewer what you learned from the experience.

If you are asked to describe the hardest decision you had to make, identify *a* hard decision.

2. What Is a Recent Risk You Have Taken?

Remember that your response should come from your own experience. Don't be stopped by the Only the All-Stars Can Play myth. No one will expect you to be a major investor risking millions of dollars on a new product design. It is helpful, although not necessary, to give an example related to the position for which you are interviewing.

Let's say, for example, that the question is asked at a sales interview. Your example could relate to the risk of being rejected at the interview. (Rejection is a common experience in sales.) You could say, "I took a risk in applying for this position because I could have been rejected. However, I want this job, so I applied. I know that I have to take chances to have a chance to get the things I want in life."

3. How Do You Overcome Obstacles?

One approach is to take a broad question like this and reduce it to *a specific example*. Think of an obstacle you confronted, perhaps recently. Describe the obstacle briefly and explain how you overcame it.

Hector answered the "obstacles" question this way.

Hector: When I was working at Smallco during the summer, I was responsible for researching the overhead costs associated with one of our products. One of the regular staff members—I'll call him "George"—refused to give me some important information I absolutely needed. At first, I was really miffed, but I kept my frustration to myself.

I started to think about ways to remove this obstacle. I wanted to avoid going to George's manager, if possible. I decided that maybe George felt threatened or insulted because a summer worker was asking for the information. So I went to George again and approached the issue differently. I asked him to help me find ways to evaluate the overhead costs. George gave me the information I needed and some really good advice besides.

4. Discuss a Problem You Have Solved.

It would be helpful to identify a situation in which you demonstrated a Positive Characteristic—a capability, skill, or attribute that would be useful in the position for which you are interviewing. For example, if you are interviewing for a position that requires people management, describe a situation in which your interpersonal skills were important. Perhaps you solved a conflict in a residence hall, motivated members of a club, or dealt with morale problems at a place of work.

5. What Aspect of a Sales Job Would You Find Unattractive?

You would probably like some aspects of any job less than others. For example, you might not like the paperwork that must be completed following a sale. In that case, you could say that you wouldn't enjoy doing the paperwork. However, *add* that you realize how important it is, so you would put all necessary energy into *doing it well*.

Bill: I am interested in a career in sales because I know it will be interesting and financially rewarding. At the same time, I know that every job has its drawbacks. The thing I least like about sales is all the paperwork. However, I know that doing it well is a necessary part of succeeding.

6. What Do You Think You May Not Like About Working for Our Company?

This is a legitimate question. It may be designed to see whether you are realistic in thinking about a firm or a job. No work situation is paradise on earth. You could mention one or two concerns you have. For example, if the firm is very large, you can express concern that individual performance may not be recognized or that competition for promotions may cause tensions with your peers. If the firm is small, you may be concerned about the possibility that promotional opportunities might be limited.

Many other things might concern you: commuting time, relocation, long hours, hectic environment, and so on. It is not unreasonable to identify these as things you "may not like." *However,* if you cite something you may not like, *add* that you are willing to do it because it is *outweighed* by the things you *would enjoy* if you worked for the company.

Robert answered the "may not like" question this way.

Robert: As I think about starting my career with this company, the thing I am concerned about is getting lost in the crowd, because this is a large firm. I work hard and I know that I will contribute to the success of the company. I know that I will have to spend time to learn the organization so that I don't feel lost and so that my contributions to the firm are noted by my managers.

7. How Did You Develop the Summary (or Objective) on Top of Your Résumé?

Many people look at different sample résumés to help them with their own. You could indicate that you looked at a number of sample summaries (or objectives), gleaned some ideas you found useful, applied them to your own situation, and then wrote your text. It is acceptable to gain ideas from samples or from discussing ideas with a counselor. However, simply *copying* a sample (or taking advice from a counselor *verbatim*) would indicate that you had not been thoughtful in constructing your résumé. Remember, it's a plus to learn from others, but a definite minus to be a mindless copier.

8. What Do You Think Makes You Stand Out from the Rest of the People I Have Interviewed Today?

Again, a legitimate question, but (as with all questions) be careful to understand its *intent.* Your basic approach should be to *stress your Positive Characteristics* and relate them to the needs of the firm. Do *not* even attempt to *put down* other people who are interviewing. You might reply, "I know you are seeing some excellent candidates today. The reason you should hire me is that I have at least three outstanding attributes you need. For example, [you can now proceed as though you had been asked "Why should we hire you?"]

9. Think of Someone Outside of Your Family Who Is a Good "People Person." Why Do You Think of the Person That Way and How Are You Similar and/or Different?

People skills are important on most jobs. If you have a person "outside of your family" who exhibits those skills, fine. Mention that person and briefly describe his or her people skills. The key, however, is to show how *you* have demonstrated *your* people skills. If you have skills similar to those of the person you are describing, mention that and give examples. If the other person has skills you don't yet have but are seeking to acquire, identify those skills and how you are striving to acquire them. If you have a "people" skill in addition to those the other person has, indicate that skill to the interviewer as well.

The Least-Loved Question

"Tell me about your weaknesses."
This least-loved of all interview questions comes up frequently. Use these strategies in your reply:

- *Don't* give the interviewer a list of weaknesses. You can't possibly be helping yourself by reciting your faults.
- Just try to avoid hurting yourself; this is a no-win question.
- Neutralize the question by using *one* of these types of answers:

  —*Classic:* State a "weakness" that is really a strength; for example, "I work very hard and usually finish my projects ahead of schedule. That's my style, but I know I can't expect that from everyone."
  —*Trivializer:* Identify something that is not closely related to the subject at hand, such as "I know I'm just not good in the natural sciences. I had to work hard just to get a B in astronomy."

- If the interviewer comes at you with *another* "weaknesses" question, stand your ground: "Are you concerned about any particular weaknesses that you would like me to discuss?" This takes the burden off your shoulders and will probably close out the "weaknesses" questions with no harm done. If your interviewer cites a possible weakness, try to show that you are actually strong in that area by citing a Positive Characteristic from your chart.
- If the interviewer cites as a *weakness* a characteristic you actually have:

  —Show that you are striving to overcome it;
  —Show how you compensate with strengths in other areas;
  —Show how the characteristic could be viewed as a strength rather than a weakness.

HONESTY: THE POWER OF TRUTH

Bill came to see me before one of his interviews. He was concerned. At a previous interview, Bill's answers about his work experience seemed to fall flat. "Maybe I could stretch a few points a little," Bill suggested. "Who would get hurt? Besides, everybody lies, don't they?"

I could understand Bill's concern, but couldn't agree with his solution. Getting a job is tough, but that makes honesty even more important. I wanted Bill to find his own answer by thinking about some questions.

"Bill," I asked him, "why do you think your responses fell flat?" Bill told me his work experience was thin. "My experience just isn't what they're looking for. I need to dummy things up a little."

"Bill, I think you have it backward," I responded. "The problem is that you weren't *honest enough* at your interview. Remember, the underlying question is the first peak: 'Why Should We Hire You?' The honest approach is to use your work experience, whatever it was, to demonstrate some of your Positive Characteristics. *You* are the subject of the question. Your work experience is really just providing examples and historical context."

Bill thought for a moment and then reasoned, "So, if I stretched the truth about my jobs, I'd be moving away from the point of the question, which is my own Positive Characteristics. By focusing my energy on identifying what I demonstrated, achieved, or learned on those jobs, I would be honest and also more successful."

"Exactly," I said. "Altering the facts lets you escape from truly examining what is important about them. The consequence of telling the truth is that you will actually identify more of your Positive Characteristics."

In this chapter, I have shown you five important facets of interviewing:

1. The structure of a typical interview and how to promote your Positive Characteristics;
2. How to use your response to the first question to set at least part of the interview agenda;
3. How to understand and use the question–answer–question cycle;
4. How to approach questions you are likely to face at your interview;
5. How to use your résumé as a source of interview practice questions, because your interviewer may use your résumé as a source of real questions.

We also looked at interview ethics and saw how honesty is both the right and the successful path.

Now it's your turn to ask questions of the interviewer.

CHAPTER ELEVEN

Asking Productive Questions

In this chapter, I will show you why your questions to the interviewer are so important and will give you two unbreakable rules for constructing them. We will examine sample questions and see why they worked.

WHEN IT'S YOUR TURN TO ASK

Hector's interviewer made a typical statement, 20 to 25 minutes into the interview.

"Well, Hector, you've been giving me some interesting answers this morning. Do you have any questions you would like to ask me?"

Hector knew he had better have some questions, because his *questions* could prove to be *more important* than his answers. Without some well-considered questions, Hector would have blown the interview!

There are at least two reasons why your asking questions is important:

- Your questions will show how seriously you have researched and thought about the *job,* the *firm,* and the *industry.* They are good indicators of how seriously you want the job and how well you prepare for business meetings.
- Your questions will show whether you apply good business sense in examining business information.

A good way to prepare your questions is to think about the *four major environments* of your career:

- Job (the function you will be performing);
- Firm (your specific employer);
- Industry (the line of business the firm is in);
- World events (how they influence the other three environments).

THE JOB

Hector came to see me before his first interview. He was confident (and correctly so) that he could handle any questions asked of him, but he wasn't sure how to ask questions of his own. I asked Hector what he wanted to know about the particular job for which he was interviewing. Hector was hoping to begin a career in financial management by being hired for the training program of a large manufacturing firm.

I asked Hector for a question he would like to ask his interviewer. "I wonder what they teach you in the training program," he replied. Hector was on to something, but I knew he had to be careful. I asked him how he would ask that question. Hector said, "How about 'Tell me about your training program.'" Good idea, bad question!

I picked up the firm's recruiting brochure and asked Hector whether it contained an answer to his question. "Yes," Hector admitted, "it describes the training program on page 3." I told Hector he had just violated Rule 2 for formulating questions for an interviewer.

Rule 1. Ask questions that are of *sincere interest* to you.

Rule 2. NEVER ask a question that has an easily accessible answer. Instead, read the available literature and ask a question that builds on what you have read.

What Hector should do is ask a question based on what he learned from reading the firm's literature. Then he could pose an *informed question* (and get an informative response).

Hector revised his question this way.

Hector: I read in your literature that the training program is 24 months long and that trainees go through four rotations. Could you tell me what skills we will be gaining during these rotations and whether we have any input into where our second and third rotations will be?

In his revised question, Hector has added an interesting dimension. Notice how he speaks of the program trainees as "we" rather than "you" or "they." By this use of "we," Hector is sending the message that he already sees himself as a part of the organization and thus encourages his interviewer to see him that way.

Hector has now asked about a subject on which he really wants more information (Rule 1) and he is building on the literature the firm would expect him to have read (Rule 2). Hector now has a double-win situation.

THE FIRM

Hector and I then thought about the second category for questions—*the firm.* Following Rule 1, Hector thought about something he really wanted to know—in this case, the firm's prospects for future growth. But Hector also followed Rule 2—he posed his question based on material he had read, rather than asking something he could easily find out on his own. This was Hector's question.

Hector: I read in your annual report that the firm's gross revenue, in real terms, has been growing steadily for the past five years. But this year, Happy Corporation and Dollarco have started to compete in some of your key markets. How does the company plan to retain its revenue growth in light of a possible loss of market share?

Through this question, in addition to getting some information about a subject he really cares about, Hector will achieve two goals:

- Showing that he can use business terminology correctly (notice how he worked "gross revenue," "competition," and "market share" into his question);
- Demonstrating that he is able to make good use of business information, sources, and data.

THE INDUSTRY

Hector reviewed his research notes and wondered about something he had read in the *Standard & Poor's Industrial Survey.* "Let's see," Hector thought, "my notes indicate that American firms are facing competitive problems because their plants and much of their equipment are not up-to-date. This firm is spending a lot on expansion, but what about modernization? Does the industry as a whole share a common perception on how to deal with the modernization problem? In this company's approach, does expansion include modernization?"

Hector was expressing some good questions to himself. He was also following the two unbreakable rules by preparing a question about something he really wanted to know and *building* on his research materials rather than asking about something he could find answered in readily available material. This is how Hector framed the actual question.

Hector: I have read that the American engine manufacturing industry in general is facing problems because much of its plant and equipment is not up-to-date. I have also read that this firm is in the midst of a five-year expansion program. Is its expansion addressing the modernization problem that typifies the industry?

By asking this question, Hector has shown two important things about himself: He has done research beyond the materials the company provided, and he can relate the company's situation to that of the industry as a whole.

WORLD EVENTS

Hector and I pooled our thoughts about a question in regard to the influence of world events on the company. This is the question Hector developed.

Hector: A good deal of concern has been expressed about the ability of American manufacturing firms to be competitive in the face of international competition from low-wage countries or government-subsidized industries. Do you foresee serious problems in that regard for manufacturers of engines in general or for your company in particular?

This question shows Hector's awareness of the importance of world events (international competition) to the company's future.

Hector had done a good job, but I encouraged him to prepare some additional questions.

HECTOR'S OTHER QUESTIONS

The Job

1. Can you please tell me how your own career has developed at this firm and whether someone entering the firm today would have similar opportunities? (This is a good question if the interviewer is a practitioner in the field Hector wants to enter.)
2. If I work hard and prove my value to the firm, where might I be in five years? (Hector should be prepared to answer the interviewer's possible response: "Where would you *like* to be in five years, Hector?")

3. I have read in your literature that the company's training program is comprised of four six-month rotations. Does the employee have any input into where he or she will go at the end of each rotation? How do you evaluate the employee's performance during the training period? (This question conveys interest and preparation.)

The Firm

4. Can you describe for me what a workweek is really like as a financial analyst for this company?
5. I have read in *Business Week* that a major competitor, Happy Corporation, is increasing its market share in your main market. What plans does your firm have to regain its lost market share?
6. I am excited about the possibility of working for this company, but I am also concerned about the turnover rate among your new hires. What accounts for the high turnover rate, and are any steps being taken to correct this situation? (Only ask a question of this type if you are sure of your facts—that there actually is a high turnover rate.)
7. What are some of the personal attributes it takes to be successful in your firm? (Listen carefully to the answer. You may then say something like: "I'm glad to hear that, because I possess just those attributes. For example, ...")
8. What are some of the skills it takes to be successful with your firm? (The hint under question 7 applies here, too.)

The Industry

9. Do you think that this company and other firms in the engine manufacturing industry will be helped by the trend toward increasing American exports?
10. *Business Week* has indicated that economies of scale in the engine industry suggest that medium-size firms like this one would do well to find merger partners, in order to stay competitive. Do you foresee fewer, but larger, firms over the next five to ten years?

World Events

11. I read in the company's annual report that about 15 percent of your revenue comes from overseas. Since 1992, has the European Community made it harder to maintain that export business?
12. Environmental concerns are prominent in America and in other industrialized countries. Do such concerns affect this company? I didn't see any mention of them in your literature or in the business press.

Don't Raise These Questions

It's important to remember that there are *some questions you shouldn't ask,* at least until you get the job offer. Do *not* raise the following questions:

- How much does this job pay? The topic of compensation should be left until the job has been *offered* to you; you don't need the information until then. The question cannot advance your objective (which is to get the job offer) but may block your getting the offer. Similarly, do not raise questions about fringe benefits and vacation time during the interview process.

  If the interviewer asks you what compensation you expect, you may respond with "What are you offering your top prospects?" If you are pressed to state a salary expectation, give a range—for example, "in the mid-$20s."

- Will your firm pay my tuition if I enter an MBA program? *Don't initiate questions of any kind about an MBA!* The implication of such a question will often work against you and won't work *for* you. Firms that think an MBA is important to your career *with them* will let you know. Some firms react negatively to MBAs. By asking the question, you may raise a concern that your *real* career plan is to work for two years and then quit to get your MBA. Furthermore, you may be giving the message that you are not serious about the job for which you are interviewing. As an example, if you are interviewing for a sales job and mention an MBA, the interviewer is likely to infer that you want an office-based job in marketing rather than an outreach job in sales.

  If the *interviewer initiates* questions about your plans for an MBA, you might respond like this: "I am very serious about my career. If an MBA is required to advance in your firm, I would discuss with my manager appropriate steps to take. There are many fine evening MBA programs designed for career people seeking to move ahead."

Thank-You Letters: Nice or Necessary?

Thank-you letters after an initial interview are nice but not necessary. In all likelihood, the person who interviewed you has made up his or her mind about you before starting work the next day. A thank-you letter is unlikely to influence a decision in your favor.

If your goal is *courtesy,* write the thank-you letter. If your goal is *impact,* a thank-you letter probably won't help.

In this chapter, you found out why the questions you ask are so important and learned two unbreakable rules for formulating your questions. I showed you how to use the four environments to help you build your questions and gave you two questions *not* to ask at your interview.

Your interview is nearing its close, so let's move on to that phase.

CHAPTER TWELVE

Asking for the Job

In this chapter, I will tell you why and how to ask for the job—if you want it offered to you.

IF YOU WANT THE JOB, ASK FOR IT!

I indicated earlier that you should go into the interview wanting the job offer. At the end of the interview, *ask for it!* It is perfectly appropriate to let people know what you want during a job interview, just as you would at a business meeting.

Imagine this scene. You are completing four years of hard work in college. You really want to pursue a career in the retail industry, and you are interviewing today with Discount Luxuries, the second largest retailer in the country. It's about 28 to 29 minutes into the interview.

Interviewer: Well, our time is up. Thank you for coming in today to discuss a possible career with Discount Luxuries.
Your reply: It's been a pleasure. Thank you.

What's missing in this dialogue? Despite your interest in the job, you simply leave the room on cue. Instead, you should close the interview by asking for the job. Let's reconsider the scene.

Interviewer: Well, our time is up. Thank you for coming in today to discuss a possible career with Discount Luxuries.
Your reply: Thank you. It was a pleasure meeting you. I want this job and I hope that you will invite me for a second interview.

Compare the two scenes. Which one will convince the interviewer that you are really interested in the job?

There are a variety of ways to close your interview by asking for the job. For example, after your thank-you, you can say, "I want you to know that I really want this job. Will you be inviting me to a second interview? [or, What's our next step?]"

It is a good idea to *practice* closing the interview with a statement of interest in the job; you will feel more comfortable doing it at the actual interview. Your interviewer will probably give you a noncommittal response (for example, "You'll be hearing from us in about two weeks"), but that's OK. He or she will take note that you had the presence of mind and the desire to ask for the job and will therefore *be more likely to invite you* to a second interview. There are at least four good reasons why you should ask for the job:

- You show the interviewer that you are interested in the job. Your sincere interest encourages the interviewer to react favorably to your interview. This may seem elementary, but it is amazingly true. When I debrief interviewers at the end of the day, they often tell me that a student's expressed interest (or lack of it) was a decisive factor.
- Many people are uncomfortable with asking for something they want. That's only natural. In order to tell someone else convincingly that you want the job, you may have to convince yourself first. This can be an asset. By the process of showing *yourself* why you want the job, you will prepare yourself psychologically to show that desire *throughout* the interview, not just at the end.
- It is easier and less threatening to like someone who says, "I like you," first. Think about your own social relationships. Isn't it easier for you to extend an invitation to someone who, you *know*, likes you. Make it easier for interviewers to like you by letting them know that *you* liked them first.
- You show that you have an appropriate degree of gumption—a necessary ingredient for success in business.

On rare occasions, an interviewer may feel that you are being too forward by asking for the job. However, because asking for the job *is usually an asset*, it is a risk worth taking.

LEARNING FROM YOUR INTERVIEW

Your answers have promoted your Positive Characteristics at your interview. Your questions have shown your seriousness about wanting the job and your ability to apply business sense. In closing your interview, you have asked for the job. Now you've finished, right? Not quite!

If you are interviewing for a sales position, asking for the job is more than important—it's critical. If you don't ask for the job, you won't get it. A salesperson has to ask for the order, not just make a presentation.

If you can't ask for the job, the interviewer will assume that you can't ask for the order.

Use phrases like these:

"I really want this job. Am I going to get it?"

"Did I get the job?"

"I want this job. When can we meet for a follow-up interview?"

Your goal *at* the interview is to be invited to a Site Visit. But you can also learn a great deal *after* your interview. As soon as you leave the interview room, find an undisturbed place where you can review the interview.

What do you want to gain from your review?

- Were there any questions that you found difficult to answer? Make a note of them so you can think about an answer for the next time they are asked.
- What did you learn about yourself rom the interview? Because most of the questions had to do with you, maybe you saw yourself a little differently or became aware of something about yourself for the first time. Make a note of that quality so that you can think it through later.
- Were any topics discussed that seemed particularly interesting to your interviewer? Make a note of them; they may come up again at a Site Visit and/or an interview with another firm.
- How did your interviewer answer your questions. *At* the interview, you asked questions to help you succeed in being invited to a Site Visit. *After* the interview, review the interviewer's responses, to learn more about the job, the firm, or the industry. This information may help you succeed at a Site Visit later.
- When you asked for the job, what did your interviewer say? In many cases, the response will be a nondescript "You'll be hearing from us in two weeks." Sometimes, the interviewer will say, "Here's my business card. If you haven't heard from us in two weeks, or if you have any questions, let me know." Make a note of the two-week time frame, to help you keep track of your interviewing progress with that firm.

Let's take a look at some of the notes that members of the Job Search Club took after their interviews, and what they gained from the experience.

Hector Keeps Improving

Although Hector realized that no one response is likely to ruin an interview, he still wanted his interview to be as strong as possible. When he got home, he thought about what he might find unattractive in being a financial analyst and wrote out this response:

I know I would enjoy most aspects of being a financial analyst, like the analytical work and the array of things you need to take into account to do your job well. On the other hand, I know that there can be strict time constraints on completing a project. Although I have demonstrated good time-management skills and work well under pressure, I can't say I really find that aspect of a job attractive. No job is perfect and I'll enjoy the other aspects so much, I know I will enjoy being a financial analyst and will do it well.

Hector had now addressed the question (cited something he would find unattractive in the job) and minimized the possibility that his response would hurt him. Hector had showed that he was capable of succeeding in the face of something he didn't like (time constraints) and that what he liked about the job far outweighed what was unattractive. Therefore, he had showed that he was both capable and eager to be a financial analyst.

THE JOB SEARCH CLUB REVIEWS THE EXPERIENCE

I encouraged all the JSC members to compile their notes by going through the interview question-by-question. What was the first question? What was my answer? How did the interviewer proceed? How did I feel about the question?

Alice followed through as I had suggested. She noted that her interviewer's first question was predictable enough: "Why did you choose to attend Emeritus College?" Alice thought about her response and felt comfortable that she had promoted some of her Positive Characteristics (academic excellence, self-reliance, communication, and leadership). The fact that the interviewer asked a follow-up question about one of her characteristics (leadership) confirmed Alice's feeling. It also helped her realize that her first response had set some of the agenda for her interview, just as she had planned. As Alice continued reviewing the interview questions, she was struck by her response to the second question about her Good Buy experience. In her response, Alice mentioned friendship as one reason her co-workers had cooperated with her. "My own capacity for making friends," noted Alice. "That's a Positive Characteristic I haven't identified for myself in the past."

Right after his interview, David also sat down to take notes. He noticed two things. First, he had felt comfortable describing himself with adjectives, rather than with a historical narrative, the way his friend Lauren did. Second, the first follow-up question in his question–answer–question cycle was about interpersonal skills. This confirmed for David that interpersonal skills were important for his career in sales.

Hector was taken aback by one of the questions he was asked in the middle of his interview. "Hector, what would you find unattractive about being a financial analyst?" Hector had been so psyched about the positives of being a financial analyst that he had forgotten to take seriously any negatives while he was preparing for his interview. "I had a hard time answering that one," he said to himself. "I'll make a note of it now and prepare an answer for a future interview when I get home."

In this chapter, you learned why and how to ask for the job before you leave the interview room. Observing some members of the Job Search Club has made it easier for you to learn from your interview experience.

Things are moving along nicely for you. You researched well and you wrote a good résumé. Your résumé earned you an interview (actually, many interviews). You learned the twin peaks of interviewing, how to research a firm, how to ask good questions, and how to ask for the job.

In the next chapter, you will see how Lauren conducted her interview with Toolco, utilizing ideas we have discussed in this section.

CHAPTER THIRTEEN

Lauren's Interview

In this chapter, we'll see how Lauren utilized what she learned in the Job Search Club to succeed at her interview.

Lauren, who wanted to be a financial analyst, came to see me the day before her first interview. She would be meeting with a representative from Toolco. Lauren wanted to make sure she hadn't overlooked something in her interview preparation.

We looked at her research chart, discussed the twin peaks questions, and reviewed what Lauren knew about Toolco. Lauren and I walked through her responses to the common and the difficult questions. Lauren had researched the firm thoroughly and had thought about questions she might be asked. We discussed the questions she wanted to ask. Her own questions adhered to the two unbreakable rules. She was going to the firm's information session that night. Was anything missing?

Lauren had prepared well. I had only one more piece of advice. I suggested that Lauren review four thoughts that would stabilize her state of mind on the morning of her interview. Some of the thoughts she already knew from our earlier sessions, but some were new. I recommend that you review these four thoughts on the day of any interview.

FOUR THOUGHTS FOR YOUR STATE OF MIND

1. Focus on your objective—to get the job offer. You can decide whether you want the job if and when it's offered.
2. Assume the best about the interviewer. Most interviewers are intelligent, well-intentioned, and intent on hiring. If your interviewer is not, there's nothing you can do about it anyway.
3. Be yourself—at your best. Don't try to act the way you imagine someone else wants you to be.
4. Remember than an interview is a *business meeting between equals*. See

yourself as a professional discussing a potential business relationship with a particular firm, not as a student taking an oral exam.

LAUREN MEETS TOOLCO

The next day, Lauren wisely arrived at the waiting room about 15 minutes ahead of her interview time (a good idea; being late can destroy your chances). Her early arrival gave Lauren a chance to freshen up in the washroom.

At 9:00 A.M., as scheduled, Mike, the interviewer from Toolco, came into the waiting room. Because he had already met Lauren at the firm's information session, they recognized each other and exchanged some friendly greetings.

Mike (extending his hand to Lauren):   Hi, Lauren, how are you? I'm glad to see you again.

Lauren (standing up and extending her hand to shake Mike's):   It's great to see you too, Mike, I really enjoyed your information session last night. Between work and the information session, you must have had a long day yesterday.

Mike: Yes, I did; but it's a part of my job I enjoy.

Mike and Lauren continued on their short walk from the waiting room to the interview room.

What follows is an abridged transcript of Lauren's interview with Mike from Toolco. Let's see what we can learn from it.

SMALL TALK

Mike: Well, Lauren, you're the first person I'm interviewing this morning. Do you like to schedule your interviews before class?

Lauren: Yes, I do. I have classes all morning and I work most afternoons, so early interviews work out best for me.

Do you find that most students you interview have a preference for a particular time of day?

Mike: Yes, but it doesn't make any difference to me. I'm not affected by the time of day an interview is held. Because of other commitments or whatever, some students want to be first, some want to be last, and some prefer to be *anything but* first or last.

Lauren: I guess the idea is to schedule an interview appointment as best you can.

Mike: Yes, I don't think there are any especially fruitful times or especially fatal times to interview.

This dialogue is a good example of handling small talk well. Mike asked about when Lauren schedules interviews, but he clearly isn't going to evaluate Lauren based on this information. He does, however, want Lauren to be as relaxed as possible, so he eases into the interview with a harmless question. For her part, Lauren addresses Mike's question and then continues the conversation with a related question of her own. Lauren has shown here that she can pick up on a small talk topic and keep the subject going. That's a handy skill in business.

Hitches and Glitches

Mike's response to Lauren's question contains some good advice. Some students drive themselves crazy trying to get the best interview slot of the day. They are sure that a particular interviewing time (first/last of day; right before/right after lunch) will give them a comparative advantage because of some supposed state of mind the interviewer will be in. I have seen various advice givers supporting almost every hour of the day as the "best," but I have never seen any evidence to support any hour as being better than any other.

If you can choose an interview time, forget all that advice. Pick a time that's best for you—a time that conflicts least with classes or your part-time job. If you can't wake up before 10:00 A.M., don't schedule an interview for 9:00 A.M. Whatever your decision, base it on your needs, not on some supposedly best time from the interviewer's point of view.

If your interview is not on campus, you will have to schedule a time that is mutually convenient for you and the interviewer. If you are interviewing on campus but your interview is scheduled without your input, what you lose is logistic flexibility, not any comparative advantage.

THE OPENING QUESTION

Mike: Well, Lauren, I'm glad to hear that you enjoyed our information session last night. This morning will be our chance to meet one-to-one. We have about half an hour to see whether there might be a good match between Toolco and you. I'm going to ask some questions to try and find out more about you, and then there will be time for you to ask some questions about Toolco.

Lauren, could you tell me why you chose to attend Emeritus College?

Lauren *(after pausing for a moment to collect her thoughts):*   Mike, when I was a senior at Hilton High, I became very serious in thinking about what I wanted to do in terms of college. I was admitted to several colleges, and, after visiting them, I decided Emeritus would be best for me. What I wanted was a good education and a good social life. In addition, I had some vague idea about needing a job some day, and I knew from people I had asked that Emeritus would give me good preparation.

I'm glad I made the decision I did. I've received a good education, both in liberal arts and business, and made some good friends.

In answering this question, Lauren followed the three principles I suggested to keep in mind:

- She *conveyed* one or more Positive Characteristics (careful preparation, balanced goals—academic, social, career);
- She cited a *significant example* of her preparation (visited various colleges, gained perspective on the business program's reputation) and did not give a trivial reason for choosing Emeritus ("The campus was pretty" or "The drinking age is 18 in that state");
- She *avoided* the *very* personal (she said that her social life was important, which is fine, but she did not go into detail about frat parties or her boyfriend).

Notice that, in Lauren's response, she has given Mike lead-ins for a follow-up question. For example, Mike might pick up on Lauren's academic interests, her overall experiences at Emeritus, or one of her Positive Characteristics. Typical of many interviewers, Mike chooses to follow up with a question about Lauren's academic experiences.

FOLLOW-UP QUESTIONS

Mike: Lauren, you mentioned that one of your reasons for choosing Emeritus was to get a good education and that you were happy with your choice. Could you tell me, what was your favorite course at Emeritus and what was your least favorite?

Lauren paused here for a moment, to collect her thoughts. She realized that Mike had asked a two-part question and that the real intent of Mike's question was to see *why* Lauren liked or disliked a course. Lauren remembered that she *wasn't* being asked to rank-order her courses, literally identifying her favorite and least favorite courses.

Lauren: My favorite course was political science. It was great because the professor really challenged us to analyze important issues like how people can be affected differently by the same law. Professor Jones also helped us express ourselves. In class, he would ask questions to help us clarify our thinking—and he made some good notes on our term papers.

On the other hand, I really didn't like my course in sociology. We had this big lecture hall led by a grad assistant. The textbook was pretty good, but I didn't get much out of class.

Lauren has done a good job with this question. She answered both parts of it, but kept her response brief. Lauren also conveyed one or more Positive Characteristics (analytical ability, communication skills) and gave good examples of why she liked or disliked a particular course. Notice that Lauren has utilized material she gathered in answering her Short Self-Profile (SSP) to help her at her interview. In her SSP, Lauren used her political science class as an example of her communication skill. Here, she adds analytical skills gained in the same class, because they are essential for a successful financial analyst.

Lauren has shown how to be honest and smart at the same time. In picking a course she didn't like, she identified a course not in her major and gave brief, uncontroversial reasons for disliking the course.

As many interviewers would have done, Mike has followed Lauren's first answer with a question related to it. What we have just seen is a brief example of the question–answer–question cycle.

Mike has decided to focus his attention on Lauren's career interests.

Mike: Lauren, you've given me some interesting answers about the academic side of your experience. I wonder, what interests you about a career in finance at Toolco?

Again, Lauren pauses a moment to think about Mike's question. She realizes that this is really the second of the twin peaks: Why do you want to work for us?

Lauren: Mike, I'm interested in Toolco because a career in finance with your firm would give me a chance to do several things I like and do well. For one thing, I like to analyze information and apply it to a practical situation. Another thing I like is the opportunity to use my quantitative

---

Process Is Paramount

There are two important things to notice in Lauren's response on her courses and throughout her interview. First, Lauren prepared for the interview and practiced interview questions, but she *did not memorize* her responses. Practice is professional, memorizing is for parrots. Second, as Mike listens to Lauren, he is trying to learn about her *thought process:* why she does things, how she deals with situations, what she likes or dislikes. Mike is not assessing every word like a scholar reviewing an ancient manuscript.

---

analysis skills and computer ability, both of which are important in finance. A third thing I want is challenge; that's very important to me.

Lauren has again followed the three principles in her response, but she has made a mistake by introducing a fine-sounding term ("challenge") when she hasn't really considered its relevance.

Lauren isn't sure whether she has answered Mike's question. Rather than continue the interview with that uncertainty over her head, she clarifies the situation.

Lauren: Mike, I've given you several reasons why I want to go into finance. Would you like me to tell you more?
Mike: Yes, I would, Lauren. You mentioned that you want a challenge in your career. What do you mean by "challenge" and can you give me an example of a challenge you have faced in the past?

Lauren said to herself: "Maybe I shouldn't have thrown in that word 'challenge' so loosely. Mike wants to know what I consider a challenge, and I haven't really thought about it before. But, no use worrying about that now. Let me think about a challenge. I would be best to get away from academic examples and give a work example."

Lauren: Well, Mike, last year I really had a challenge on my summer job. I took a job with Smallco, a medium-size firm about 40 miles from here. I wanted the challenge of working in a corporate environment—I had taken previous jobs based on where I could save the most money for school. I also wanted the challenge of living away from both home and college. It was an important experience because I learned a lot about how things really get done in a firm. I also learned to be more comfortable living on my own.

Lauren has recovered well from her loose talk about "challenge" and has given Mike some good material to follow up—especially about what Lauren learned at Smallco. She has also let Mike know about her ability to live independently—a helpful Positive Characteristic because working for Toolco would require relocating.

> Lauren wasn't expecting a question about "challenge." Like Lauren, you will probably have at least one question you don't expect. Your interviewers will be interested in your thought process and will probably try to find something to ask which, they believe, you haven't practiced. Don't worry:
>
> - If you have done your work in the early chapters of this book, you should have plenty of good material to utilize. What Lauren did was take an example from the first twin peak (Why Should We Hire You?) and modify it to be an example of challenge.
> - Even if your answer isn't as good as you would like, no one answer is likely to make or break your chances of success at your interview.

Mike: Lauren, that was an interesting example of a challenge. Following up on that, I wonder if you can tell me more of what you learned at Smallco, or on other jobs, that would help you succeed at Toolco.

Mike has done exactly what Lauren wanted. He has followed up on Lauren's Smallco answer with a question linking her experience at Smallco with a possible future at Toolco. Mike's question really belongs to the first of the twin peaks: Why Should We Hire You?

Lauren: You know, Mike, the main thing I learned at Smallco was that, even in the corporate world, things don't work out with textbook efficiency. For example, I was working in the accounting department doing accounts payable. I noticed that we were billed for widgets twice within a short period of time. I discussed it with my supervisor, and, to make a long story short, we found out that the purchasing department had accidentally overordered widgets because of a miscalculation by an inventory clerk. Somehow, I used to think that private businesses didn't make mistakes—that everything worked smoothly. In reality, you can have a snafu a day, although I'm glad to say that, at Smallco, people tried to make sure particular mistakes weren't repeated.

In this response, Lauren conveyed one or more of her Positive Character-istics (a sense of corporate day-to-day reality; attention to task). Her exam-ple was significant: it came from an actual work situation where Lauren experienced an important reality. Lauren *did not* fall into the Only the All-Starts Can Play trap by trying to inflate her example into something monumental or newsworthy. Interviewers do not expect that you are a captain of industry, but they do expect your answers to be honest and believable.

Lauren had some additional examples, but she wasn't sure that Mike wanted to hear them. Instead of clogging her head with doubt, she asked Mike.

Lauren: Mike, I gave you just one example. Would you like some more examples?

Mike: No, Lauren; I'd like to hear more, but our time is running short. Besides, you've already given me some examples of your strengths. I'd like to ask you about the flip side. Everyone has weaknesses. Lauren, can you tell me about your weaknesses?

Lauren (pausing a moment):   Well, as you say Mike, everyone has their weaknesses. For example, I know that sometimes I just work too hard. I get my projects completed before they're due. I know that I have to be careful not to expect that same degree of work and efficiency from everyone.

Lauren has taken the classic approach to a "weakness" question that we discussed in Chapter 10. She has identified a "weakness" that is really a strength. Notice that Lauren has kept her answer brief. This is especially important in responding to a no-win question—one that at best, you can only neutralize. Questions about "weaknesses" or things you didn't like belong in that category. In addition, Lauren has blunted possible concern by indicating that she can't expect "that same degree of hard work and effi-ciency from everyone." That is an important statement. Some employers worry about hiring workaholics because they can drive their other staff members crazy.

In this interview with Lauren, Mike decides to see what Lauren would do if *pressed* on the "weakness" question.

Mike: Lauren, that was an interesting example, but you gave me a weak-ness that is really a strength. Can you give me an example of a weakness that would limit your effectiveness at Toolco?

If Mike had just asked for another weakness, Lauren was ready to respond with the Trivializer, like only getting a B in Chemistry. But Mike has specified "a weakness that would limit your effectiveness at Toolco." Lauren knows that no one can win this question, so she decides not to expose herself to potential problems by identifying more weaknesses.

Lauren (with a sincere smile on her face): Mike, I'm not exactly sure what you mean. Are there any potential weaknesses I might have that concern you? I'd be glad to talk about anything you mention.

This response by Lauren is both polite and professional. Quite appropriately, it puts the burden on Mike, not Lauren, to identify possible weaknesses of concern to Toolco.

Mike: Well, Lauren, one thing I'm concerned about is your ability to deal with some of the pressure you'll experience. Some of our finance managers can be very demanding and rather pointed in their criticisms.

Lauren: I know what you mean, Mike.

Lauren actually chuckled as she thought about the example she was about to give Mike. A sincere, natural chuckle is fine; a contrived, forced chuckle is not.

Lauren: Last summer, at Smallco, I had one manager like that. His name was George. He was gruff when he asked for things and usually found some fault in anything we did. Whatever he wanted was due yesterday. But I learned to deal with it by not taking George's behavior personally.

The funny thing is, we went to a staff lunch at the end of the summer. George was more than pleasant; he was a ball of laughs. That experience helped me learn to separate professional relationships from personal ones.

With this answer, Lauren has addressed Mike's question about her ability to withstand pressure. Mike's concern has probably been reduced or eliminated.

About five minutes were left in the half-hour interview between Mike and Lauren. As most interviewers would do, Mike asked Lauren whether she had any questions for him.

Lauren has avoided a common blunder in her response about dealing with pressure. Some students would have said horrendous things about George and would have described the pressure at Smallco as unbearable. Even if true, this is usually a poor tack to take. Avoid criticizing a former employer: it makes you sound like a malcontent, and it can introduce a tone of negativism into the rest of your interview.

Notice how Lauren stated the facts about George, to give her response context, but didn't belabor her problems with George. To the contrary, she pointed out that George was really a nice person and that she had learned the important distinction between professional and personal relations. (Understanding that distinction is in itself a Positive Characteristic.)

QUESTIONS FOR MIKE

Mike: Lauren, you've given me some interesting answers to my questions. I wonder if you have any questions for me. Since you were at our information session last night, maybe you don't.

Lauren knew full well that she had better have some good questions to ask, even if she *was* at the information session.

Lauren: Thank you. Yes, I do have several questions, Mike.
I'd like to ask you about something the chairman said in Toolco's annual report. Mr. Wright was talking about the problems medium-size companies sometimes have keeping their production facilities up-to-date without heavy borrowing. Then Mr. Wright mentioned that Toolco would finance most of its modernization from current revenue. Given the amount of capital needed, do you think the chairman's goal can be achieved?

Lauren has asked about one of the four basic environments—the company.
With this question, Lauren has shown Mike that she has done her research, has thought about what she has read, and has related a general company issue, modernization, to her specific career interest, finance. As she will do with all her questions, Lauren has followed the two unbreakable rules. She has asked about a subject in which she has a sincere interest,

and she has built on what she has read, rather than asking something that could be readily answered from available sources. For example, Lauren *didn't* ask: "Does Toolco plan to modernize its production facilities?" or "How does Toolco finance capital improvements?"

Mike: That's a very good question, Lauren. Yes, we can achieve the goal of financing modernization without heavy borrowing. In fact, our next annual report will show that all of this year's capital investments came from current revenue flow.

Lauren listened to Mike's answer with interest. She knew that she should acknowledge Mike's response in some way before asking her next question. Lauren also knew that it would be a good idea to ask about another of the four basic environments. For her next question, Lauren chose the job.

Lauren: Mike, I'm glad to hear that Toolco is meeting its objectives in regard to financing modernization. It sounds as though Toolco has a good handle on its financial controls. That's especially interesting to me, with my goals in finance.

Mike, let me ask you a question about Toolco's Financial Management Program. I think I have a good understanding of the FMP from the recruiting brochure and your information session last night. But I'm unclear about the mix between hands-on assignments and classroom work. I'm also curious as to whether we would be involved in the finances of the modernization program while we're still in the FMP.

Mike: Those are good questions, Lauren. In the first year, about a third of your time is in class, with a special emphasis on accounting and financial controls at Toolco. After the first year, you have fewer hours of classroom work, but the classes are more advanced and tend to relate to specific issues you'll be dealing with in your second year and after you complete the program. Of course, when we talk about the mix of time, we may be talking about 60 hours a week.

In regard to the modernization, that's a main issue at Toolco for at least the next five years. You'll be spending plenty of time on it.

Lauren again listened to the answer, to make reference to it in some way before she asked her next question. Lauren also realized that, because Mike referred to 60 hours a week, she should make sure to tell Mike she's ready to do whatever it takes to succeed at Toolco.

Lauren: I appreciate your explanation about the classroom/hands-on mix. I'm most excited about the hands-on assignments, but I know from speaking to current FMPs last night that the classroom work really does tie into our work assignments. By the way, I heard about the 60 hours a week last night, too. I want you to know, Mike, that hard work and long hours don't bother me. In fact, I've been working part-time most semesters, so I'm really used to it already.

Mike, if we have time, I would like to ask you a third question. I read in *The Wall Street Journal*, and also in the *Standard & Poor's Industry Surveys*, that the tool industry is concerned about imports from Asia and about being blocked from exporting to Europe because of the new EC structure that started in 1992. Is this a concern for Toolco? Foreign markets weren't mentioned in Toolco's annual report.

With this question, Lauren acknowledged Mike's previous answer, clearly stated her willingness and ability to work long hours (it doesn't hurt to convey a Positive Characteristic), showed that she had researched beyond Toolco's recruiting literature and annual report, and related her research to both the general tool industry and external events, two more of the four basic environments. That's quite a bit—and all in one question!

Mike: That's another good question, Lauren. In the past, Toolco didn't discuss foreign trade issues much, because we thought our domestic customer base was secure and we didn't export much. We're beginning to recognize, as your question implies, that it's a new ball game now. Toolco will have to deal with foreign competitors at home and will need to export.

Lauren, did I answer your question?

Lauren: Yes, you did, Mike. I wonder, do we have time for another question?

Mike: Well, no; I'm sorry, but we don't, Lauren. I've really enjoyed our discussion, but our time is up. (Mike stands up.) Thanks for coming in today. I appreciate your interest in Toolco.

CLOSING

Lauren (standing up and extending her hand to Mike): I've enjoyed meeting with you, too, Mike. I'm really glad I had this opportunity to speak with you. I was excited about Toolco before, but I'm even more excited now.

Mike, I hope you're going to invite me to a Site Visit. What's our next step?

Mike: Well, Lauren, I'm going to be reviewing all my notes this evening. I've seen a lot of good candidates at the various colleges I've visited, so I know I'll have some tough choices to make. But everyone will be hearing from me in two weeks, one way or the other.

Lauren: Thanks, Mike. I'll be looking forward to hearing from you. I hope it's good news.

Mike: Thank you, Lauren. Good luck.

In her closing, Lauren didn't just leave the room. She expressed continued (actually, increased) interest in Toolco and expressly asked for an invitation to a Site Visit. As we would expect, Mike's response was noncommittal. Still, Lauren's closing cost her nothing and might influence Mike's decision a little in her favor.

In this chapter, you saw an abridged version of an interview. Lauren reviewed my four thoughts before her interview, to help her achieve the right state of mind. As the interview unfolded, you experienced how Lauren answered Mike's questions, conveying some of her Positive Characteristics with each response, and you saw a brief example of the question–answer–question cycle.

You saw how Lauren *asked* questions that adhered to the two unbreakable rules and were related to the four environments. You noticed how Lauren acknowledged Mike's answers before asking her next question.

Finally, you saw how Lauren closed by asking for the job.

It will come as no surprise that Lauren really impressed Mike and was invited to a Site Visit at Toolco.

Site Visits are our next topic.

PART FIVE

Into the
Home Stretch

CHAPTER FOURTEEN

Site Visits

In this chapter, I will tell you about Site Visits and whether you should accept invitations to them. I will point out three key similarities to your initial interview and five important differences. We will see what types of questions are special to Site Visits and how you need to fine-tune your own questions. I will describe your Site Visit logistics and how to avoid glitches.

A COMPANY IN ROBERT'S FUTURE?

About two weeks after the beginning of on-campus recruiting, Robert was getting to be a mailbox watcher. Every day, Robert checked for letters from any of the firms with which he had interviewed. A very impressive business envelope was there one Wednesday. Robert opened it quickly, with equal amounts of fear and expectation. The letter invited Robert to a site visit at the Omaha office of Sam Sanderson & Company, a major public accounting firm. After Robert calmed down and returned from the ceiling, he had to decide what to do next.

What's in a Name?

Robert was invited to a Site Visit, Gabrielle went to an Office Visit, and Alice went on a Second Interview. These are three different names for the same thing: an invitation to visit a potential employer's place of work, usually an office or factory, for an in-depth interview process that may last an entire day.

Robert called me to share the good news. After congratulating him, I suggested that Robert call the firm *immediately* to set up a date for his Site Visit. I had two reasons for my urgency:

- I wanted Robert to have his Site Visit *as soon as possible.* Unfortunately, when students pick a late date for their Site Visit, they sometimes find that all the positions have been closed before the day of their visit.
- I wanted Robert to arrange a date that would least interfere with his course work.

If your first interview is like the first date, then your Site Visit is like the invitation by your Significant Other to come and visit the family. You're not talking about marriage yet, but you know that he or she must really like you, to take the risk of showing you off to the rest of the family. In the same way, a firm invites you to a Site Visit because your original interviewer thought you should be introduced to the rest of the company.

Before ending our phone conversation, I suggested that Robert come to see me, to review some basic strategy for his Site Visit.

The first thing I wanted him to know was that there are similarities and dissimilarities between a first interview and a Site Visit.

The three key similarities are:

- It's still an interview process. People you have never met will ask you questions, and you will ask them questions.
- It's still a business meeting between equals. The firm will evaluate you as a potential employee; you will evaluate the firm as a potential employer.
- It's still necessary to try to convince the firm that it should hire you. The people from the firm will want you to feel that their firm is the right place for you to start your career.

There are also five important areas of differences:

- The Site Visit structure;
- The Site Visit questions;
- Your recent research;
- Your fine-tuned questions;
- The Site Visit logistics.

Let's take a detailed look at each of these important differences between the Site Visit and your first interview.

STRUCTURE OF THE SITE VISIT

Typically, a Site Visit will last for the better part of a workday. You will interview with three to five people; each of them will have input into the decision to make you an offer. Your first interview may have been only

30 minutes, but during Site Visits each interview may take 45 minutes to an hour.

SOME NEW SITE VISIT QUESTIONS

By the day of a Site Visit, you will have had more time to think about what you want from a job in general and from working for that firm in particular. Therefore, you can expect to be asked questions like "How will you evaluate your job offers to determine which one you will accept?"

In a way, this question is flattering because it assumes you will have two or more offers. But that is not the point of the question.

Its real point is "What are your important values, which will be critical in evaluating a job offer?" This is a more sophisticated version of "Why do you want to work for us?," which you were probably asked at your initial interview. (Robert's evaluation, in Chapter 17, gives a good approach to answering this question.) (Some interviewers ask this question even at an initial interview.)

Who Else Are You Seeing?

Another new question you may be asked at your Site Visit is "Where else are you interviewing?" or "How are your other Site Visits going?"

Firms ask this question to find out who their competition is and to see whether there is any focus to your interview process.

Let's assume that Robert has more than one Site Visit scheduled. Robert could say, "I'm scheduled to visit with several other public accounting firms, for example, X and Y"; or, "I am very fortunate to have been invited to several other Site Visits. The visits I've had so far seem to have gone well."

There is no need to make a long response to this question. Robert has let his interviewer know that other firms are interested in him. If you are *pressed* to name the other firms, I would name them in a matter-of-fact way. However, if the question makes you feel uncomfortable or put-upon, you could say, "I'm very glad to be *here* today. As you know, I'm very interested in your firm. It's not clear to me why you're asking about these *other* firms." Remember, an interview *is a business meeting between equals.* You have every right to let the other person know when you feel that a question is too intrusive.

What if Robert has been invited to only one Site Visit? (Remember, always be honest—never lie and never shade the truth.) Robert could say, "This is my first Site Visit, and I'm very excited because your firm is my number-one choice"; or, "This is my first Site Visit; I'm waiting to hear from several more firms." In all likelihood, the number of Site Visit invitations you receive overall will not influence any particular firm's decisions in your regard. There is no need to be worried about this question, but you should be prepared for it.

At a Site Visit, you are likely to be asked "what-if" questions. These are designed to see how you think through situations and problems.

What-If Questions

Sometimes, at an interview, you are asked to deal with situational questions. These questions are often, but not always, framed in a "what-if" mode:

What would you do *if* an employee whom you are managing is performing up to standard but not up to his or her abilities?

What would you do *if* a proposal you have worked on for over a month is severely criticized by your manager?

It is often a good idea to frame some "what-if" questions for yourself as you prepare for an interview. Think about situations that might arise in the profession you are aspiring to enter. Here are some examples:

- Conflict or confrontation between manager and subordinates—What would you do if a subordinate with many years of experience told you a decision you made was simply wrong? What if he or she says the decision was foolish and lame-brained? What if these things are said in the presence of other employees?
- Conflicting demands on your time—What would you do if you are scheduled to meet with a prospective new account that has limited business potential and your largest existing account calls and demands to meet with you at the very same time?
- An erroneous report—Assume that you have given your manager a report on revenue projections for your division, to be used in a presentation to the board of directors. You then discover that you have made an error that affects the *amount* of the revenue projected but not the *direction* of revenue growth. Your manager calls you 15 minutes before the board of directors' meeting, to see how things are going in the office. Do you tell your manager about the error you discovered?

YOUR RECENT RESEARCH

Sometimes you will be asked at a Site Visit about your research *since* your initial interview. The question might be phrased: "Robert, can you tell me

---

Answering What-If Questions

Answer in terms of the process you would follow to solve the problem:

- What would you need to know?
- What would be your priorities?
- What external interests would you have to consider?

This is how Bill answered the question about conflicting demands on your time:

Bill (after pausing to collect his thoughts):   There are several things I would need to know to solve this conflict. First, can I get either client to change appointment times without risking the loss of their business? If not, my own priorities would be to satisfy the existing, large client because it's important to be pragmatic. I assume I'm being paid on total business, not new customers. However, I have to take the firm's interest into account. Is there any reason why the potential client is more important than I think? Perhaps we need to gain exposure with clients in their field of business.

---

what you have learned about our firm since your first interview?" If you have done some *additional* research since the first interview, you have shown serious interest in the firm. If not, perhaps you are not serious, or perhaps you go to meetings without being up-to-date in your preparation. Make sure that you have researched current articles in the press about the firm and/or its industry.

FINE-TUNING YOUR QUESTIONS

Remember how you prepared questions you wanted to ask at your initial interview? You will need to utilize that same process to prepare questions for your Site Visit. However, at a Site Visit, your questions must be more finely tuned, to address the areas of interest and the responsibility of the person interviewing you.

Sample Questions to Ask at a Site Visit

At a second interview, you will typically meet with three to five people. They are likely to hold different levels of positions in the firm or may come from different functional areas. It is important, as you interview with each individual, to ask questions relating to *that person's* area of professional interest. The sample questions in Table 14.1 show how you might ask different questions of different individuals.

David's Dilemma

David had mixed emotions when he came to see me. He had done everything we had recommended in the Job Search Club and had succeeded in being invited to three Site Visits. He was happy about two of them, but concerned about the third.

"Schlockco just isn't for me," he said. "The more I think about it, neither the firm nor the industry is for me. But I convinced them at the on-campus interview that I really want the job, so I don't want to feel like a liar now. And I'd love to visit San Diego. What should I do?"

I told David that he had raised an important issue and that students struggle with the same question every year. Only he could decide whether to go, but I gave him my guidelines for deciding whether to decline a Site Visit invitation.

- *"No Way!" "Really?"* If you are 100 percent sure, positively and absolutely, that there is no way you would accept a job from that firm if offered, then don't go. If there is the slightest possibility that you might want the job, then go to the site visit.
- *Remove needless concerns.* David, for example, had told the firm at his initial interview that he wanted the job. In the context of that interview, David was telling the truth. Now he has a different perspective. At this stage of the process, it is not unethical to change your mind.
- *Don't count birds in the bushes.* I told David not to turn down the visit to Schlockco on the assumption that one of the other firms he had interviewed with would make him an offer. There is no job offer until the firm has explicitly made it to you. Praise for your character, capabilities, and potential with the firm is not a substitute.
- *The interviewer is not the firm.* Don't reject a Site Visit because you didn't like your interviewer. A half-hour experience with a single individual is no basis for closing out a potential career opportunity.

Table 14.1   Some sample questions to ask at a site visit.

For a person who has joined the firm just recently

What did you learn in college that is helping you do your job at X Corp.?

Why did you choose X Corp.? Do you feel comfortable telling me why you preferred X Corp. to other firms?

What is the most or least satisfying part of your job?

How does your position relate to other functions at X Corp.?

Is your position at X Corp. what you expected it would be?

Where do you see yourself at X Corp. in three to five years?

Do you socialize with other employees at X Corp.? Are the other employees here friendly with each other outside of work?

How would you describe the atmosphere at X Corp.? Is it formal or informal; serious or relaxed; structured or unstructured?

For a person with senior management responsibility

How is your firm positioning itself to deal with the current economic slowdown?

What does it take, in terms of outlook, skill, and determination, to be a manager with this company?

Why do clients choose your firm instead of your competitors?

I read recently that a major challenge facing firms in this industry is _____. How does X Corp. plan to meet this challenge?

What skills or attributes do you look for in your staff when you are evaluating their potential for promotion?

How does your position [functional area] relate to other positions [functional areas] at X Corp.?

In terms of the decision-making process, would you describe it as centralized or decentralized? How much autonomy do *you* have, for example?

If you make a sound decision that results in a worse-than-anticipated outcome, will you be evaluated more on the soundness of the decision or on the disappointment of the outcome?

For a person who works in an area (e.g., engineering; marketing; store; headquarters) not directly a part of the area for which your are interviewing

What are some of the challenges you face in [your division or function]?

What do you enjoy most or least?

In what ways does [your function] work along with [my function]? Are there any aspects of the relationship you would like to see improved?

How has your [area] changed over the past four years or so?

SITE VISIT LOGISTICS

The logistics for your Site Visit are usually more involved than for an on-campus interview. On campus, you probably went to your friendly Placement Office, signed up for an interview time that was arranged around your class schedule, and then interviewed in a cozy interview room in a familiar college building.

For your Site Visit, the logistics will be different in three main ways:

- You will arrange for your interview date through a corporate person whom you've probably never met;
- You will probably have to travel and stay overnight, perhaps in a strange city;
- You may incur expenses, most of which will probably be reimbursed.

A Site Visit may cause you a lot of anxiety: it is a new experience, and you are getting close to a job offer. I advise you to handle your logistics smoothly, to keep this aspect of your job search from *adding to* your anxiety. Try these tactics:

- Contact the firm to arrange your visit as soon as you receive your letter of invitation. In that way, you'll have the best chance of scheduling a date that is least disruptive to your regular agenda.
- Clarify the nitty-gritty arrangements when you schedule your visit:
  —If travel is necessary, does the firm plan to make the arrangements (e.g., send you a prepaid ticket) or will you need to arrange your own travel?
  —If you will be staying overnight, has the firm prearranged a hotel accommodation or should you make your own reservation?
  —Will transportation from your hotel to the firm on the interview day be provided by the firm?
  —If you need to make any of these arrangements yourself, how will reimbursement be made?
- Three days before you leave for your Site Visit, *confirm* your date and review your travel and overnight accommodation plans with the person the firm has designated as its liaison.
- Establish a wake-up assurance system for the day of your interview:
  —Ask the hotel to give you a wake-up call that allows you plenty of time;
  —Set the hotel alarm clock and/or bring your own travel alarm;
  —Have a trusted friend or relative call you.

If you arrange this wake-up system, you won't worry all night about waking up on time in the morning. The friendly call from a trusted person may help to calm your nerves.

THE JOB SEARCH CLUB'S QUESTIONS

I reviewed these simple guidelines with our Job Search Club and, as always, invited questions.

Gabrielle: My Site Visit is in Lincoln City, which is only two hours away. Do you think it's really important for me to stay in a hotel the night before?

Richard: Yes, I do. Let me tell you why:

- It's good for your peace of mind:
  —It's best to wake up in the city where your interview will be held. You'll feel more corporate and less like a student.
  —You don't have to worry the night before about travel glitches like flat tires or snowstorms.
  —You can take a walk or do something else to relax yourself before your long day of interviewing begins.
- It's good for your body. You don't have to wear yourself out traveling at the start of your interview day.
- Because you don't have to travel far, you can review your twin peaks of interviewing before your day-long business meeting between equals begins.

Gabrielle: But I already scheduled my Site Visit and we never discussed a hotel. What should I do?

Richard: Remember the Plowman's Principle? Identify your goal, then say "How do I achieve it?" You want to stay overnight in Lincoln City. Call your contact at the firm and say something like this: "Denise (or whoever), I'm really looking forward to my visit to your firm next week. One thing we didn't discuss was hotel accommodations. I'll need to stay in Lincoln City the night before we interview. Can you help me with the cost of the hotel?"

Almost always, the firm will say "yes." They want your interview to be a success and they don't want to appear cheap. The key is for you to ask.

Gabrielle seemed satisfied, so we continued on with Bill.

Bill: I'm going to be interviewing with some sales managers in San Francisco. I've never been there. Do you have any special advice for me?

Richard: Yes, you have raised an important point. I would do some research on San Francisco, for two reasons. First, you'll feel more comfortable when you get there. Second, you want your interviewers to know that you're serious about the job. Researching a location will tell them you are serious enough to learn about the living realities in a new city.

Site Visit Travel List

Clothing (for dressing without distress)

- Travel in one suit, pack another. You may be taken to dinner with someone from the firm the night before the interview—directly from the airport. If you're afraid of spilling something, pack two suits.
- Dress shoes; for women, comfortable medium-heel pumps;
- Several clean shirts or blouses; minimal and tasteful daytime jewelry;
- Socks and underwear; for women, unpatterned, neutral-color hosiery;
- Belt, several ties; for women, a manageable size purse—not the one you've hauled to class all year;
- Handkerchief.

Toiletries

- Shaving equipment; for women, daytime makeup;
- Deodorant (unscented);
- Toothbrush, dentifrice, mouthwash;
- Shampoo and hairdryer.
  (If you forget any of these, you may be able to acquire them at a big-city hotel, for an extra charge.)

Accessories

- Travel alarm clock;
- Folder or briefcase (to hold materials you bring with you and materials firms may give you).

Résumé and transcript (in case someone on your interview schedule doesn't have them readily available).
Letter of invitation (names, times, directions, and details it contains might be confused or forgotten; keep it with you as an anchor).

Bill: How should I do this research?

Richard: Let me suggest several sources:

- The Chamber of Commerce of the place you are visiting;
- "Job Search Guides to (wherever)" usually have a section about the business and social environment of the city—we have some in our career library and they are available in many bookstores;
- Local newspapers (e.g., *The San Francisco Chronicle*) can give you a good feel for current news in that city—our college library periodicals room gets newspapers from all over the country.

Lauren: I know about the myth of the ten-foot-tall interviewer, but I'm still concerned. On campus, I interviewed with Melanie from the human resources department. She was young and I had met her the night before. This time, I'll be meeting *real* corporate executives. Aren't they going to be at least eight feet tall?

Richard: (I had to chuckle. If we could only get the interviewer's size down to 5'11", we'd have it made.) I know what you mean, but the same realities of life apply to people at headquarters and to Melanie. They're people who brush their teeth, have headaches at work, and eat hot dogs at home. Some of them just hold more important corporate positions. Remember, at some point in the past, they were in your shoes, coming out of college looking for a job. In the future, you may be in their shoes.

David: What should we bring with us to the Site Visit? For example, how many suits?

Richard: That's a good question. You might want to use our Site Visit Travel List so that you don't forget anything. If you're visiting a part of the country that has a different climate, check national weather maps a week or so before your interview, for an idea of the temperature range there.

Expenses

Hector: Richard, what about expenses? Who pays for what, and what records do we need to keep?

Richard: That's a good question, Hector. Remember, you should be thinking about yourself as a professional. Professionals are reimbursed for their reasonable, legitimate professional expenses—and they're not shy about asking for it. Let's look at some major categories.

    Transportation: In your case, Hector, Manufacturco is sending you plane tickets for the round trip. Some firms will tell you to arrange your own transportation and give them the bill. If you're going by plane,

Hitches and Glitches

Thank-you letters. Unlike the on-campus interview, a Site Visit should be followed up with a thank-you letter. Remember:

- The offer/no-offer decision takes a while, and your written, courteous statement of interest *may influence a decision* in your favor;

- Your letter may be giving an impression of you to people who may be your future co-workers, mentors, and managers.

At a minimum, write to the person who invited you to the Site Visit. If possible, write a thank-you letter to all the people you meet during the day. (I wrote to each of the nine people who interviewed me for my current job and I'm a happy, well-employed person today.)

Lunch. If you are at the Site Visit for the whole day, the firm will take you to lunch as a guest (or invite you to the employee cafeteria).

- Order something you know you like and can eat easily. Dripping tomato sauce from spaghetti or launching airborne pieces of crab shell will not help your case.

- Put your food, not your foot, in your mouth.

No matter what the firm tells you, lunchtime counts in your evaluation. Your lunch companion will be asked what he or she thinks of you, even if the comments never appear in writing. Avoid controversial subjects like politics or religion. Don't be critical of anyone you meet, even if your companion is.

Expenses. Make sure you are clear, before you leave for your Site Visit, what you'll need to pay for out-of-pocket. In that way, you won't be caught short of cash if you need to pay for a cab, a toll, parking, and so on. Be sure to collect and retain your receipts to present for reimbursement. You will avoid delay and needless friction over amounts to be reimbursed.

Love thy neighbor. The other people interviewing for the same job are future colleagues, not competitors. You will be evaluated on how you get along with your peers, not how you put them down. Be careful of your attitude and actions toward your peers.

you'll probably need to charge the tickets. Save your credit card slip and air ticket receipt for reimbursement. By the way, it's usually a good idea to have a travel agent arrange your flight. If you don't have a credit card, don't be reluctant to explain that to the firm and ask that the tickets be sent to you.

If you drive a long distance to the Site Visit, make a note of the mileage for the trip. You'll be reimbursed on a cents-per-mile basis. Save and present your toll and fuel receipts. The firm will pay for these costs because they are reasonable and legitimate. The firm would probably not reimburse you for oil or antifreeze you buy in connection with your trip.

Hotel or Motel: Some firms prearrange a hotel for you. If the firm you're visiting does not make the arrangement, choose a moderately priced accommodation near the site. Again, a travel agent can be helpful. Usually, incidental expenses like telephone calls and pay-TV are your responsibility, but the firm will pay for the room.

Meals: Most firms will reimburse you for meals associated with coming to or leaving the Site Visit. Save your receipts. You should order something reasonable—not a hot dog from a corner stand, but not a royal banquet either. The firm will pay directly for any meal at which you are a guest.

Same-Day Offers

Robert: Richard, should we expect to get a job offer at the end of the day?

Richard: That's a good point, Robert. Let's consider the possibilities. *Probably, you won't.* The logistics of the situation limit the possibility of getting a job offer on the spot. Each person who interviewed you will write an evaluation. Then all of those evaluations of all the candidates will need to be reviewed. There's usually not enough time while you're there to make a decision on a job offer for you. Many firms will not make their decisions until *all* the candidates can be interviewed. Don't worry if you don't get an offer at the end of the day. However, you should clarify when you can expect to hear from the firm about an offer.

In a minority of cases, you will get an offer at the end of your Site Visit. You can then jump for joy, shake the person's hand, and express your happiness. But *do not accept* the job on the spot. (We'll discuss this more in Chapter 16.)

In this chapter, you have learned how and why to arrange Site Visits; what about them is similar to an interview and what is different; how to prepare and succeed at your Site Visit.

In the next chapter, you will taste the fruit of your hard work: a job offer.

CHAPTER FIFTEEN

Your Job Offer

In this chapter, I will tell you about job offers—why you get an offer and what an offer letter generally says; how to juggle decision dates without losing a job offer; and how multiple offers add leverage to your bargaining power but sometimes mess up your head.

AN OFFER OF MARRIAGE?

An offer letter is extended by a firm only after serious consideration of how well you match the firm's needs. Is there a match in an absolute sense, between you on one hand and the job on the other? Is there also a match in a relative sense? How good is the fit between you and the job when compared to other applicants?

Generally, a firm that offers you a job thinks there is a good match between you and the job in *both* an absolute and a relative sense. The hard work you put in throughout your life, to *develop* your Positive Characteristics, and the hard work you put in during your job search, to *identify* and *convey* them, has paid off in a professional employment opportunity.

To follow the social analogy we've been using, your initial interview was like a first date; your Site Visit was an invitation by your Significant Other to meet the family; your offer letter is an offer of marriage.

It is a compliment to receive an offer letter, but you can still take the compliment and not accept the job, as we discuss further in Chapter 17.

WHAT AN OFFER LETTER SAYS

A letter from a firm offering you employment is serious business. The letter will generally state at least these three things:

- The firm is offering you a job, usually identified by job title, function, or department;

- The date the firm wants you to start;
- The compensation package, for example, ". . . at an annual compensation of $25,000 plus health insurance and two weeks' vacation."

In addition, an offer letter may include some or all of these four information items:

- The location of the job, for example, "Our facility in Seattle" or "Our office in San Antonio";
- A sentence or two telling you how to respond (send a letter of acceptance, sign a copy of the offer letter, or call and confirm in writing);
- A decision date—the final date the job will be held as yours to accept or reject (after that date, the firm no longer has any commitment to you);
- A contingency statement—the offer of employment may be contingent on any or all of the following:
  —that you graduate from your college by a certain date;
  —that you submit an official transcript;
  —that you have made no false representations to the firm during the interview process;
  —that you will provide proof of your employment eligibility in accordance with the Immigration Reform and Control Act of 1986;
  —that you pass a general physical;
  —that you pass a drug test.

QUESTIONS ABOUT OFFER LETTERS

At the weekly meeting of the Job Search Club, several members brought in copies of offer letters they had received. After congratulating them, we decided to make offer letters our topic for discussion and questions.

The Case of the Leaky Letter

Alice began by asking about the content of offer letters.

Alice: What if the offer letter is missing something like a job title, starting date, or compensation?

Richard: Alice, if it's missing one of those three items, something is wrong. I would contact the person who signed the letter and ask for a written clarification. It's important to have a written understanding of the basis of the offer, to reduce the chances of unpleasant surprises later.

In terms of the four items that *may* also be included, if there is any doubt about location, method of response, or decision date, call the person who signed the letter and ask for clarification. Then send a brief thank-you letter restating the clarifications made.

On the other hand, if the firm makes none of the contingency statements I indicated, don't go fishing for them. Contingencies weaken, rather than strengthen, your offer.

Juggling Decision Dates

Hector: Richard, I received an offer letter from Happy Co. It's a good offer, but I've got a problem. The job I really want is with Manufacturco. I was at the Site Visit yesterday, but I won't hear from them for about three weeks. Meanwhile, my response to Happy Co. is due in ten days. What should I do?

Richard: First, congratulations, Hector. You worked hard to get that offer, and I hope you're pleased with your success. Now, let's see what some other club members think.

There were a number of suggestions. They generally fit into one of two categories: Stall and Lie. We began our discussion by diagramming a time line that represented the situation facing Hector. (See Figure 15.1.)

According to the basic Stall approach, Hector could call Marie Antonelli (the person who signed his offer letter) at Happy Co. and ask for more time to give them his decision. At a minimum, Hector needs to push back his decision date (DD) for Happy Co. until after he's expecting to hear from Manufacturco. In our diagram, we moved the Happy Co. decision date to March 22.

A corollary tactic was to call Jim Flores, who had invited Hector to the Manufacturco Site Visit. Hector could tell Jim that he was being pressed for a

Figure 15.1   Hector's time line problem.

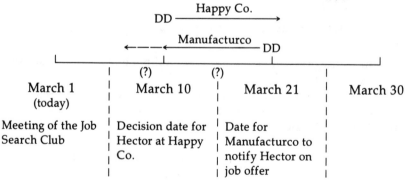

decision by another firm and that Hector was deeply interested in Manufacturco but couldn't give up a job-in-hand for one he hoped for. Under the circumstances, could Manufacturco let him know earlier—say, in ten days—whether he would be getting an offer or not? This corollary part of Hector's Stall plan was represented by a reverse arrow going to March 10 and on, possibly, to March 7.

If Hector became successful in both parts of his plan, he would know where he stood with Manufacturco before he had to respond to Happy Co. If *either* tactic worked—Happy Co. gave him 12 more days (to March 22) to give them his decision, *or* Manufacturco gave an offer/no-offer response in 10 days or less (by March 10 or earlier)—Hector would know where he stood with both of these firms before he had to make his decision on Happy Co. As it turned out, each firm accommodated Hector only partially, but that was enough to meet Hector's needs.

Hector's Two Calls

As with many business situations, *how* you say things is very important. Hector wanted to juggle his decision dates without losing the job offer from either Happy Co. or Manufacturco. This is what Hector said when he called Marie and Jim.

Hector: Hi, Marie? This is Hector Sanchez. How are you?

Marie, I'm calling about your letter; I received it today. I'm excited about getting a job offer from Happy Co., but I have a problem with the decision date and I hope you can help me with it.

I'd like to finish my interview process before I respond to any offers. I should be finished in a little more than three weeks. Can you extend Happy Co.'s decision date to the end of March?

Marie: I'm glad you're excited about the offer, Hector, and I understand your reasons for wanting to push back your decision date. Unfortunately, there is no way I can accommodate you by waiting for your answer until the end of March. The *most* I can do is extend your decision date one week, until March 17.

Hector had planned for this contingency—a partial accommodation—before he even picked up the phone. One option would be to ask Marie to extend an extra week, to March 24. But Marie seemed to say that the one week addition was the absolute outside decision date for Happy Co.

Hector: Thank you, Marie. I appreciate your extending my decision date until March 17. I would have preferred March 24, but I understand the constraints you're under. You'll be hearing from me soon.

Hector noted on his time-line chart the new decision date for Happy Co. He also wrote a brief thank-you letter to Marie, confirming the new decision date of March 17.

Hector's next step was to call Jim Flores at Manufacturco. Because Marie was able to give Hector a partial accommodation, Hector needed only a partial accommodation from Jim. He would then know where he stood with the two firms before making a decision. This is what Hector said to Jim.

Hector: Hi, Jim? This is Hector Sanchez. How are you?

Jim, I want to thank you for inviting me to a Site Visit at your San Diego facility. The people there explained that they will be extending offers on about March 21, the day after the last candidate's Site Visit is scheduled.

Jim, you know how enthusiastic I am about Manufacturco. But I have a problem and I hope you can help me with it. I have an offer from another firm. I already got them to extend my decision date to March 17, but they can't wait for an answer any longer than that.

Manufacturco is my first choice, Jim, but I can't take a chance of losing the other offer while I'm waiting to hear from your firm. Is there any way Manufacturco could let me know before March 17 whether it will extend me an offer? I really need to know one way or the other before then.

Jim didn't want to lose Hector, but he couldn't give Hector a response on the spot. After checking out the situation in San Diego, Jim called back and told Hector he would be hearing, one way or the other, by March 15. Hector sent Jim a brief note to thank Jim for his efforts and to confirm that Hector would hear about an offer by March 15.

Hector's main goal in juggling dates—finding out whether he had an offer from Manufacturco before he responded to Happy Co.—had been achieved. Notice that Hector:

- Expressed his continued interest to both Marie and Jim;
- Made no threats about not accepting an offer, but merely requested help in addressing his problem;
- Was honest: he told Marie he was excited about the offer from Happy Co., which was true; he did not say Happy Co. was his first choice or anything else that was not true;
- Sent thank-you notes to Marie, confirming Happy Co.'s new decision date, and to Jim, regarding Manufacturco's revised date for notifying Hector whether he would receive a job offer.

SHOULD HECTOR HAVE LIED?

One of the Club members suggested: "Lie, Hector! Just say 'Yes' to Happy Co.; that way, you'll be sure to have a job. Then, if Manufacturco offers you a job, call Happy Co. and then tell them you've changed your mind. You've got to look out for yourself first!"

Although Hector had decided to proceed with the Stall approach, the Job Search Club agreed to think about the ethics of the Lie approach for our next club meeting. (A summary of the Club's discussion is in Chapter 17.) Both Hector and I oppose the Lie approach.

After our discussion of Hector's Happy Co./Manufacturco dilemma, the Job Search Club continued its discussion about offer letters.

GET IT IN WRITING

Bill: I have some good news. My offer from General Thrills is in the bag.

Richard: Congratulations, Bill; but what do you mean, "in the bag"?

Bill: Well, Larry, the district sales manager in San Francisco, told me he really likes me and he's going to hire me. We even discussed salary, bonus, and use of a car.

Richard: Bill, that's great. Exactly what did your offer letter say?

Bill: Well, I don't have an offer letter yet. Larry said I should be getting it soon.

Richard: Bill, you don't really have an offer until you get it *in writing.* I suggest that you don't turn down any other offers, at least until you receive a formal offer letter on General Thrills stationery.

A STAB IN THE BACK

Alice: I'd like to ask a related question. Let's say we do get a formal offer letter and accept the offer. Can the firm back out on it?

Richard: Alice, that's a good question. According to the Principles for Professional Conduct of the College Placement Council: ". . . Employing organizations are responsible for the information supplied and commitments made by their representatives . . . ." It is extremely rare for a firm to revoke a written offer, unless the job applicant fails to meet up to a contingency expressed in the offer letter. I surveyed college placement professionals on the East Coast recently, and the results confirm how rarely an offer is revoked.

Firms don't make hiring decisions lightly, and revoking an offer would hurt a firm's reputation for years to come.

Still, I want you to understand that a firm could revoke its offer, probably without legal penalty. In fact, a firm could fire you on your first day of work. It's not at all likely, but it could happen. We'll discuss this more at our next meeting, when we deal with the Lie approach that someone suggested to Hector.

Lauren: I received an offer letter from Toolco, and I'm happy with it. Why not just say "Yes" and be done with it? Frankly, this job search stuff takes a lot of time and energy.

Richard: That's a valid comment, Lauren. The ultimate decision is up to you. But, before you decide on your next step, I would like you to understand how offers add leverage in your job search process.

WHY TWO IS FOUR TIMES BETTER THAN ONE

Richard: Unless you are absolutely, positively, beyond a shadow of a doubt, 100 percent certain that Toolco is the firm you want to marry, it's too early to say "Yes." I'll give you three reasons:

- Some people are so *relieved* when they get their first offer, they interpret their happiness about *an offer* as happiness with the firm. I suggest that you wait at least a few days before saying "Yes," so you can sort things out in your head.
- You haven't made your Follow-up Visit to Toolco yet. [That's our topic in Chapter 16.] Only after you have visited again, with your offer in hand, can you make a decision based on the best available information.
- If you do say "Yes" to Toolco, you are honor-bound to call the other firms still considering you and withdraw from the job search process. But if you do that, you'll be choosing Toolco without knowing your options.

There is another advantage to having at least two offers. It leverages your bargaining power because your choice is between Firm X and Firm Y, rather than between Firm X and no job. From that position, you are better able to negotiate things you might want: a higher starting salary, an earlier salary review, a more convenient starting date, or a position in a more desirable division of the company. No results can be guaranteed, but it can't hurt to strengthen your bargaining position.

Free agents in major league baseball offer an example. If the Cardinals are the only team interested in Player X, he has little bargaining power. His choice is between the Cardinals and being out of baseball. But if the Mariners also make an offer, Player X is in a much stronger position to bargain for contract terms he wants. In baseball, the difference can be hundreds of thousands of dollars; for you, the difference may be only a few thousand dollars. However, for any given job, more money is better than less.

Offer Letters and Your Head

Offer letters often have an impact on how you see yourself. If you receive many offers, it's a boost to your ego. If you receive no offers, you may get down on yourself. It's a good idea to put the situation in perspective, so these feelings don't get out of hand.

It's nice to get offer letters, but getting three, for example, does not mean that you're three times a better person than if you had only one, or three times better than *someone else* who gets only one. Similarly, getting no offer letters doesn't make you a zephyr who needs to "get a life." Offer letters have a pragmatic meaning in the employment marketplace. The number of offers you get may reflect your job search skills, but it certainly doesn't reflect on your worth as a person.

David: Richard, are you saying that it's always better to get multiple offer letters? Usually, there's a down side to everything, at least for some folks.

Richard: You're right, David. A lot of times in life, an opportunity is either good or bad, depending on what you do with it. For some students, getting multiple offers is more a source of dread than a source of joy. Let's take the experience of Jill, from last year's graduating class, as a case in point.

A CURSE OF MANY BLESSINGS

Jill, an English major, had three job offers: one in publishing, one in sales, and one in the retail industry. When she came to share the news with me, tension and concern were in her face. "Maybe she didn't get the offer she wanted," I thought to myself. But that wasn't the case.

"I've got three great offers," she said. "Now what do I do? I've been good at selling myself at interviews, but now I've got to switch to deciding. No matter which job I choose, I've got to give up two others."

Jill was focusing on what she would have to give up instead of what she was getting. To get Jill away from that frame of thought, I went back to our social analogy. "Jill, suppose you were getting married. Would you focus on the joy of entering a potentially wonderful relationship with a man you love, or would you be counting all the other guys you couldn't go out with anymore?"

"I see what you mean," Jill said. "It's like what they say to the parents of the bride: 'You're gaining a son, not losing a daughter.' Still, Richard, how do I decide?"

I told Jill—and this year's Job Search Club—that we would discuss two important steps in making a decision about job offers: the Follow-up Visit and Evaluating Job Offers. Those are the topics of our next two chapters.

Hitches and Glitches

To make the discussion of juggling decision dates easier to follow, I temporarily left out an important step: your Follow-up Visit, which is the topic of Chapter 16. To simplify the narrative, I presented Hector as being fully ready to decide between Happy Co. and Manufacturco if he simply knew whether he had offers from both firms. But this would be the case only if Hector *knew,* 100 percent for certain, that he wanted the Manufacturco offer more. In actuality, Hector should try to visit both firms *again,* to get a better sense of the working environment and to ask any necessary questions, without the pressure of trying to get a job offer. In Hector's case, I recommended that he try to visit Happy Co. *again* before March 17 (his new decision date for Happy Co.) so that he could clarify his feelings about the Happy Co. offer. In this scenario, it would be optimal for Hector to also visit Manufacturco again, between March 15 and March 17. Unfortunately, logistic constraints might preclude Hector from optimizing his situation.

In this chapter, you have learned what an offer letter contains, how to juggle decision dates, and what multiple offers can do *for* you and *to* you.

In Chapter 16, we will look at your Follow-up Visit—a critical but often neglected part of the job search process.

CHAPTER SIXTEEN

Keep on Running: Your Follow-up Visit

In this chapter, I will give you three important reasons why you should make a Follow-up Visit to the firm *after* it has made you an offer.

THE DREAM JOB—OR IS IT?

Alice came to my office all smiles. She had *the* offer from *the* firm. She just wanted me to know. Alice had wanted a job with FASBIE & Co., a large public accounting firm, since she was a junior. Now she had the offer! I joined Alice in her joy and congratulated her to the hilt. Then I innocently asked Alice when she was planning to go back to the firm for a Follow-up Visit.

Alice looked at me as if I couldn't be for real. We were talking about FASBIE & Co.! Who needed to visit again? I encourage a Follow-up Visit for several reasons, but I shared just the first reason with Alice at that moment. "Alice, I think it's great that you have the FASBIE offer. I know how much and how long you've wanted it. I still think you should go back again. Take a look at the physical surroundings again, see how people are working when they don't expect a visit, and try to talk to some folks you couldn't see when you went for your Site Visit. While you were interviewing, you were under pressure and you quite correctly put all your energy into succeeding at the interview. There may be some things you'll experience differently or more clearly if you go back now, when you are much more relaxed and know you have nothing to lose."

I gave Alice two steps to follow, to arrange her Follow-up Visit:

- Alice telephoned Diane Jenkins, the person at FASBIE who had signed her offer letter, to say that she was excited about the offer but she wanted to visit FASBIE again before giving her response.

- Alice let Diane know what she wanted to accomplish with her Follow-up Visit: to see FASBIE's work environment again, to speak to a sample of FASBIE employees she hadn't met yet, and to review with Diane the substance of her offer.

Alice was skeptical, but she decided to arrange a return visit to FASBIE; she was planning to be in Omaha that Friday, anyway.

On Monday, I saw Alice and asked, "What's new?" Alice looked at me sheepishly and said, "Well, I decided not to accept the offer from FASBIE & Co." "Really! Why not?" I asked.

Alice told me that, when she visited FASBIE again, she noticed that employees were sitting at clean desks, except for what they were working on at the moment. "I can't work like that," Alice said slowly. "I'm a slob. I like to have all my stuff all over the place. Besides, everybody seemed so formal and serious. It was like nobody was having any fun." Alice went on to tell me that she was considering an offer from Sincere & Olde, another large public accounting firm, instead. "But I think I'll visit them again before I give them my answer," said Alice resolutely.

Alice's story illustrates *the first of three big advantages* of making a Follow-up Visit:

1. You get a chance to see the work environment at a time when stress and your concentration on interviewing don't block out what you experience.

Alice actually reversed her decision. Her visit to FASBIE & Co. turned a "Yes" into a "No, thank you." But the trip would have been just as important if it had *merely confirmed* Alice's thinking. You should make your job acceptance decision based on the *best information* you can have *at the time.* Otherwise, you're liable to have the same problem that Rhonda did.

WILL YOU HAVE ANY REGRETS?

Rhonda called about three years after graduation, to make an appointment to see me. I was glad to see her, but I sensed that she was in some kind of trouble. When we sat down to talk, my worries were confirmed.

"Richard, I just don't know what to do," she said with some agitation. "Do you remember how excited I was to get that offer from Big Ticket Department Stores a few years ago? Now I'm not so sure I did the right thing in starting my career there. My office is closing in on me, my new boss is a bear, and I'm beginning to resent all the late hours. How did I ever decide to go to Big Ticket in the first place?"

I knew what Rhonda was going through. The problem really wasn't just the office, the boss, or the hours. Most of us experience those problems at some point in our career. We can get through those tough times if we know why we're there in the first place—and that was the key for Rhonda. She accepted her offer from Big Ticket without taking the last major step: making a Follow-up Visit. She had not made sure that any decision she made was based on the *best information available at the time.* When everything hit the fan three years later, Rhonda's feeling was "How did I ever get into this company in the first place" instead of "I made a good decision three years ago. I knew there would be tough times. I'll put my energy into dealing with the situation and not be plagued by the doubt that I never should have come here."

Rhonda's case teaches a *second* lesson:

2. Make that Follow-up Visit. *At the very least, it will be good for your peace of mind.*

IMPROVING THE TERMS OF YOUR OFFER

It is much easier to get a "Yes" to a request for a higher salary when you are speaking with the negotiator face-to-face. Think of this in a business context. Aren't most people more likely to say "Yes" to a sales presentation if it is made face-to-face rather than on the telephone?

This was Bill's situation: He wanted a job with Dollar Data as a market researcher, and succeeded in getting a job offer from them. But he wondered whether he could request a higher starting salary. "You can always ask," I told Bill. "Just make sure that you do it in the right way."

Bill's experience illustrates a *third* point about Follow-up Visits. Although negotiating is often difficult for people, especially students, to deal with:

3. You may be able to improve the terms of the offer (get more money for you!).

Here are the steps I recommend for asking for a higher starting salary:

- Don't be afraid to ask. The *worst* that can happen is that the firm will say "No."
- Try to discuss salary face-to-face when you make your Follow-up Visit to the firm.
- Ask for a higher starting salary *only* when all other issues are settled. Be ready to say, "I really want this job. If you can increase your salary offer to $28,000 [or whatever amount], I'll accept the offer right now."
- Have solid reasons for the firm to increase its salary offer to you.

Bill and I planned how to carry out the steps. Bill's first concern was that the firm would think he was "pushy" if he asked for a higher starting salary. "Bill," I told him, "making money is the American Way. No one will think less of you simply because you request more money." "OK; but what if they *do* get angry and withdraw my job offer," Bill continued. I told Bill not to worry about that possibility. In over 11 years as a placement director, I have never heard of a firm withdrawing an offer because a student asked for more money. But remember to ask in the right way!

Bill summed up this issue himself:

- It's not pushy, rude, or impolite to seek an improved compensation package;
- It won't cost you your job offer, but remember to ask in the right way.

To arrange a face-to-face meeting, Bill telephoned Jack Temple, the person at Dollar Data who had signed Bill's offer letter. Bill told Jack that he was excited about the offer but wanted to clarify the situation by visiting again. Jack was glad to hear from Bill and the Follow-up Visit was set for the next week.

When Bill visited Dollar Data again, he had none of the anxiety of his previous visit. After all, he now had the offer in his pocket and no one was going to take it away.

At the end of his visit, Bill sat down with Jack to discuss the day's events and Dollar Data's job offer. Everything about the job was clear and satisfactory to Bill (location, starting date, responsibilities, title), and he wanted the job. Only the starting salary stood in the way of his giving an immediate "yes" to the offer. This was his strategy:

- Bill told Jack that he would say "Yes" if the salary offer were increased. In this way, Bill made it clear that Jack would not be embarrassed by further demands, or a rejection of the job offer, if Jack sought to get a raise for Bill.

Hitches and Glitches

Expenses—Some firms will pay for reasonable expenses of a Follow-up Visit, but many will not. *Still,* ask to schedule a Follow-up Visit and ask the firm to cover expenses. If you ask in a professional way, the worst that can happen is that the firm will say "Yes, visit us again, but no, we can't help with the expenses."

Happy, not haughty—Sometimes a student comes to a Follow-up Visit with a haughty attitude. His or her behavior says, "Look at me, everyone. I'm here! I'm terrific! Now I'm going to decide if I want your firm in my life."

Such behavior probably won't cost you the job offer, but it will cost you *good will.* Losing good will will put cracks in the foundation of your career.

More money—Remember, you need to be sure you'll say "Yes" if the firm agrees to increase your salary. (Read Chapter 17 before you arrive at your Follow-up Visit.) Also remember to practice how you will ask for more money. "I will accept this job *only if* . . ." is a *threat* not to accept the job, and threats can hurt you. "I will definitely accept this job *if* . . ." is a promise from you that *cannot* hurt your prospects.

Learning and living with "No"—In our narrative about Bill and Dollar Data, Bill didn't get an answer about increased compensation at this Follow-up Visit, but was given a "Yes" a week later. However, what if Jack had told Bill "No" face-to-face?

When Bill and I discussed this possibility, before he went for his Follow-up Visit, this is what I suggested to him. First, think about the possibility that Jack will say "No." Then, at least, you won't be surprised. Second, remember you're discussing money, not love. If Jack says "No," it's not an attack on your character or self-worth. Third, plan how you would respond to Jack. I suggested something like this: "Jack, I'm disappointed about the response to my request for an increase in starting salary. If you had said "Yes," I would have said "Yes" on the spot. But I understand there are constraints. I'm still interested in the job and in Dollar Data. I'll let you know if I can accept your job offer within a week or so."

People who follow this advice:

Avoid the awkwardness that a face-to-face "No" can cause;

Feel better about themselves;

Feel better about the firm.

- Bill gave sound business reasons why he should get a higher salary:
  —He had a higher offer from another firm;
  —He had polled his classmates and determined that most people offered a similar position would be receiving more money;
  —Bill wasn't exactly a new hire: he had had some related experience during a six-month co-op with another firm.

Based on Bill's reasons for a higher starting salary and his statement that he would say "Yes" if his salary were increased, Jack lobbied Bill's case with his boss. The firm didn't want to be offering uncompetitive salaries—and they didn't want to lose Bill. Jack called Bill a week later and amended Dollar Data's offer to include a higher salary. Bill, true to his word, accepted the new offer. Jack and Bill agreed that they would now mutually confirm the acceptance of the amended offer, in writing, without delay.

Bill had been successful in increasing his starting salary because:

- He *asked for the increase in the right way.* He said he would definitely accept the job if his salary were raised. Bill *did not threaten* to reject the job if his request was turned down.
- He presented sound business reasons why he should be paid more. He didn't whine about the salary offer or focus on his personal needs.
- He summoned up the courage to ask for the raise; he overcame his fear of hearing the word "No."

The firm could still have said "No" to Bill, but he lost nothing by asking.

In this chapter, you learned three reasons for visiting a firm *again,* after it has made you a job offer: a nonstressed chance to see the working environment, greater peace of mind, and more money for you.

In the next chapter, we'll see how some members of the Job Search Club evaluated their job offers.

PART SIX

The Winners' Circle

CHAPTER SEVENTEEN

Evaluating Job Offers

In this chapter, we will see how two members of the Job Search Club evaluated their job offers using two different methods. We will also see how to accept a job offer "in good faith" and with no regrets.

THE LADY OR THE TIGER?

Do you remember the dramatic story of the Lady and the Tiger? In brief, a young man can choose to open one of two doors. Behind one door is the woman of his dreams. If he opens that door, they will get married and live happily ever after (at least the man will). Behind the other door is a tiger. If the man opens *that* door, he will be ripped to pieces and die at the claws of a ferocious beast. In the story, the man doesn't know which door is concealing which fate.

For many students with more than one job offer, making a decision between (or among) job possibilities makes them feel like the man in this story. The feeling is understandable: Making any important decision can be frightening. But, in real life, choosing between offers is not like choosing between the lady and the tiger:

- Your career is involved, but your *life* is not at stake. Seldom does a corporate "lady" guarantee lifelong bliss, and there is no corporate "tiger" that turns its employees into chopped steak.
- You have visited each employer and researched each firm. You should have a fairly good sense of what's behind each corporate "door," at least as it affects your early career.
- If your choice is that hard to make, it is really a choice between two "ladies." If a "tiger" were lurking, you would probably eliminate that option without much difficulty.

> To retell "The Lady and the Tiger" from a career search perspective:
>
> A graduating college senior had to decide which of two doors to open. Behind one was a lovely individual and behind the other was a lovely individual. The senior knew the two people behind the doors and liked them both. Which one would make the better marriage partner?

EVALUATING AND COMPARING OFFERS

Throughout this book, I have referred to a social analogy. At one stage, I compared saying "Yes" to a job offer to accepting an offer of marriage. To continue the analogy, one way to evaluate a job offer is to assess the degree to which it satisfies things that are important to you in a job—just as you will someday assess a potential spouse based on the degree to which he or she satisfies what is important to you in a marriage partner. My Corporate Marriage Partner exercise will give you a relatively objective way to make your decision.

THE CORPORATE MARRIAGE PARTNER

One way to evaluate a job offer is to determine the degree to which the position fulfills the criteria that are important to you. My Corporate Marriage Partner exercise will help you:

- Identify what decision criteria are important to you;
- Rank your priorities;
- Assess the degree to which a particular job satisfies your important criteria.

There are four steps for you to follow:

1. List the criteria that are important to you in a job. There is no minimum or maximum length for your list. (Some common criteria are given on page 198.)
2. Divide *100 points* among the criteria on your list. The more important a criterion to you, the more points you should assign to it.
3. Evaluate the degree to which the job offer you are considering meets each of your criteria. Assign a value from .00 (doesn't meet the criterion *at all*) to 1.00 (meets the criterion completely). Consider this your "fulfillment quotient."

4. Multiply the allocated points from step 2 by the number in step 3 (your "fulfillment quotient"). Then add the products of your multiplication to determine your evaluation of the job offer according to the criteria that are important to you.

ROBERT'S EVALUATION

Robert followed the four steps I have just described. His worksheets are given below.

Step 1. Important Criteria

Things That Are Important to Me in a Job
Compensation
Location
Starting date
Career mobility
Comfort with co-workers

Step 2. Allocation of 100 Available Points

Criterion	Allocated Points
Compensation	25
Location	30
Starting date	10
Career mobility	20
Comfort with co-workers	15

Steps 3 and 4. Assigning Final Values

Robert *had* received a job offer from Sam Sanderson & Co. These were the values he gave to the offer, based on his criteria.

Criterion	Allocated Points	×	Fulfillment Quotient	=	Point Values
Compensation	25		.95	=	23.75
Location	30		.50	=	15.00
Starting date	10		1.00	=	10.00
Career mobility	20		.70	=	14.00
Comfort with co-workers	15		.20	=	3.00
Grand total					65.75

Robert was surprised at this result. "It looks like a failing score," he said to me.

"If the answer seems uncomfortable to you, re-examine the first three steps," I suggested.

- Is your list of important criteria *accurate* and *complete?*
- When you divided the 100 points, did you accurately *rank* your criteria and give each criterion an appropriate number of points?
- When you assessed *the degree* to which a particular job offer meets your criteria, did you assign appropriate weights?

Robert looked at his chart and concluded that two changes were in order. First, "location" was no longer as critical to him as it had been initially. Robert reduced the allocated points for "location" to 15. "Comfort with co-workers" was given much more weight by Robert now. He raised that allocation from 15 to 30. Next, Robert reconsidered why he had assessed the degree to which Sam Sanderson & Co. met that criterion at .20. Upon reflection, Robert decided that he had been comfortable with his peer group and actually had been turned off by only one of the managers he met. Robert raised his assessment to .80. Based on his reexamination, Robert now ranked Sam Sanderson & Co. at 85.25.

Some Common Important Criteria

Compensation	Size of employer
Location	Corporate culture
Products	Starting date
Security	Comfort with co-workers
Promotional opportunities	Mobility
Weekly work routine	Skills used

Your list may be longer, shorter, or completely different.

Robert also had an offer to work as a financial analyst at Toolco. Robert applied the Corporate Marriage Partner exercise to the job offer from Toolco. He had no trouble listing the important criteria or dividing 100 points among the criteria on his list. (For any given person at a particular point in life, the criteria and the allocation of points to them should remain the same, irrespective of the particular job being evaluated.)

Evaluating the degree to which the job offer met his criteria was difficult for Robert, just as it will be for you. This is how Robert assigned values to each of his important criteria.

Robert: *Compensation:* In terms of salary, Toolco would start me at about $2,000 less than I expected. On the other hand, over the long term, my potential earnings are very high. I think I'll rate this a .90.

Location: Toolco moves you around, so I don't really know where I would be working a year from now. I don't like uncertainty, but maybe a year from now I'll feel less concerned about being far from home. I'll be starting in Pleasantville, which isn't great for a social life; I probably won't have time for one anyhow. I'll give this a .70.

Starting date: It's after Labor Day, just what I wanted. This will be my last long summer vacation until I retire. On the other hand, my cash situation is a bit weak. An earlier start would put some needed cash into my pocket. Let's say .85.

Mobility: Upward mobility within Toolco is great. I've seen the firm's data on that. But the firm doesn't release data about where people go if they leave Toolco. On balance, I'd say .70.

Comfort with co-workers: I loved everyone I met. A great bunch of people. A clear 1.00.

When Robert multiplied his allocated points by his fulfillment quotients, his point values for Toolco were:

Compensation	22.5
Location	7.5
Starting date	8.5
Career mobility	14.0
Comfort with co-workers	30.0
Grand total	82.5

Robert looked at each step again. He was comfortable with both his important criteria and his allocated points. (If he had wanted to make a change, he would have had to adjust these two steps for Sam Sanderson & Co. as well.) Robert checked his fulfillment quotients for Toolco and again felt satisfied; no changes were called for. Robert was now able to compare his evaluation of Toolco with his evaluation of Sam Sanderson & Co.

Important Criteria	Sanderson	Toolco
Compensation	23.75	22.5
Location	7.50	8.5
Starting date	10.00	8.5
Career mobility	20.00	14.0
Comfort with co-workers	24.00	30.0
	85.25	84.5

Both firms scored well, but Toolco had a .75 edge over Sanderson. Did that mean Robert should accept Sanderson's offer? Not necessarily.

The Corporate Marriage partner exercise is designed to identify important criteria in a job and the degree to which any given offer fulfills each criterion. It is not a precise scientific test or a sporting event where the highest score wins.

Robert could see that:

- Both jobs had considerable appeal;
- Both firms would give Robert most of what he wanted in terms of compensation and starting date;
- Neither firm held much appeal for Robert in terms of location;
- Robert anticipated better career mobility by starting with Sanderson but more comfort with co-workers at Toolco.

Based on this evaluation, which job offer did Robert accept? Stay tuned until later in the chapter. The important question for the moment is: If you were Robert, what decision would you make and why?

ALICE'S EVALUATION

Alice came to see me in December, just before finals. In her hand were offer letters from two prominent public accounting firms, Newhouse Price and Sincere & Olde. She had made a Follow-up Visit to each firm, submitted each offer to the Corporate Marriage Partner exercise, and remained equally interested in both firms. What should Alice do?

I asked Alice what time she typically woke up on a weekday morning:

Alice: I have an 8:30 class. So I get up at 8:15, wash my face, get dressed, walk from my apartment to Wisdom Hall, buy a coffee and doughnut from the concession stand, and go to class.

It was interesting to get this picture of student life, but I realized that I had really meant to ask something different.

Richard: Alice, next year, what time do you expect to wake up when you're working?
Alice (laughing):   Well, I guess I'll have to get up at 7:15 or even earlier to make the rush hour commute to Lincoln City. What a drag!

Good Morning?

Richard: OK, that sounds realistic. Now let's imagine that it's 7:15 A.M. on Monday during your fifth month on the job. Your alarm goes off. Let's say you're working for Sincere & Olde. How do you feel?

Alice: Basically, I feel good. I have friends at work, and I'm learning every day. The work is not interesting, but I feel that I'm building a solid foundation for my professional future.

Richard: Now let's change the scene a little bit. Everything is the same, but, when the alarm goes off, you're employed by Sam Sanderson & Co. How do you feel?

Alice: I'm ready to go to work, but I'm not excited. I'm going to feel very professional in that firm, but somehow I just won't feel like me. Somehow, I'm not sure that I fit in.

Richard: Alice, this "good morning" exercise is hardly scientific. In fact, it's totally subjective. But how you anticipate you're going to feel after five months on the job says something about how you feel right now. It's a feeling you should take into account. Let me tell you my own secret career story.

CONFESSIONS OF A HAPPY MAN

My career path has been different from most people's. I started out with an administrative job in academia. I felt I had reached a dead-end and decided to earn an MBA at night, in order to make a transition to a corporate career. While earning the MBA, I took what was supposed to be a short-term job in placement at a college in New York. I made it clear to my employer that my purpose in taking the job was to make contacts that would help me make the transition to a corporate career.

The year I was to receive my degree, I interviewed with a number of potential employers. One said to me, "Richard, a job with us is not for you. You're technically qualified and well-prepared. But, I've looked at your face. When you discussed your job in placement you were animated and enthusiastic. When you discussed working for us, you gave the right answers, but didn't show the same enthusiasm."

At first, I was disappointed. Given the goals I had set for myself, I had just been "rejected" for the perfect job. But, as time went on, I realized the wisdom of the interviewer's remark: Sometimes the best way to evaluate a job is to sense how joyful you feel when you discuss it.

Now, 11 years later, I am still happy when I wake up to go to my job as a college placement director. I can't imagine that I could have been as happy anywhere else. This doesn't mean *you* should work for a college or university. My story does suggest, however, that your subjective feelings when evaluating a job may be as important as your objective calculations.

Hitches and Glitches

"What do I do if my decision tools give me an uncertain answer?" That's an important point. The tools I've given you, and any others you could read about or devise, help you decide by *clarifying your decision criteria.* They can't make the decision for you.

Let's return to Robert's decision. Did he accept Toolco's offer or the offer from San Sanderson & Co.?

He chose Sanderson. Robert's thinking was this: "These are both good opportunities. But, in the long run, Sanderson has more to offer me. If I do well at Sanderson and on the CPA exam, I can be certified as a CPA in three years. That's a good credential to have, and it may be especially important for a liberal arts major to have a recognizable credential. The experience I gain at Sanderson will include making lots of client contacts in different industries. Experience, contacts, and credentials should add up to good career mobility.

"I know I'll be giving up something in terms of comfort with my co-workers, but that's a price I'm willing to pay.

"On balance, my choice is Sanderson."

LIES, GOOD FAITH, AND AN UNCERTAIN WORLD

The Job Search Club met to discuss Hector's Happy Co./Manufacturco dilemma. Hector told us about his success using the Stall—juggling decision dates. A discussion about the Lie approach was still in order.

When the meeting began, I asked the Club to give Hector rationalizations for lying—accepting Happy Co.'s offer while really intending to work for Manufacturco if it subsequently offered him a job as well. These are the comments Club members made.

Alice: Hector, be realistic, this situation means nothing to the firm, but it means a lot to you. Happy Co. can always get another employee, especially in a tight market. It's not so easy for you to get another job.
Bill: That's right! You've got to watch out for yourself. No one else will.

Gabrielle: Besides, Hector, think about the social analogy Richard is always making. Let's say accepting the offer from Happy Co. is like saying "Yes" to a proposal of marriage. So what! Engagements are broken and people get divorces all the time.

David: That's right; if you're not going to be happy at Happy Co., everybody is better off if you don't start there at all.

Lauren: Not only that, Hector. Let's be real. Happy Co. would dump you tomorrow if they wanted to. What's sauce for the corporate goose is sauce for the student gander.

According to the rules of our Job Search Club, the students were not necessarily stating their own opinions, but they certainly had raised some formidable points for Hector to consider. Hector thought about the situation. He had already proceeded with the Stall approach (see Chapter 15), but Hector was eager to tackle this intellectual and ethical challenge. This is a summary of how Hector responded to his Club-mates.

Hector: You've certainly given me some interesting rationalizations for the Lie approach. In fact, I thought about some of them myself before I saw that, for me at least, the Stall worked. Everything you've said has some surface appeal, but I'll tell you why I can't accept it.

I know it feels like a very uneven situation. The Big, Powerful Corporation against Little Ol' Me. But that's a little unreal. Yes, they can always get another employee, but probably at the cost of additional time and money to find someone. Once they think they've hired me, they notify the other applicants that the job is filled. So, to open the search again *is* a problem for the firm. And it's a problem for the other applicants, who've made decisions based on the belief that the Happy Co. opportunity was closed.

I know about looking out for myself. I'm a "big boy" and I'm aware of reality. But if I look out for myself *only*, with no regard for the interests of others, what kind of person would I be? I want to be successful, but not selfish.

The social analogy has been giving me the hardest time. If the "holy state of matrimony" can be so conditional and temporary, why make such a big deal out of a job offer?

You know, Jeannette and I are engaged, so the social analogy really hits home. When Jeannette said she would marry me, I hope she meant it. I hope she wasn't thinking, "Yes, unless I get a better offer." We both realize that our marriage may not last forever, but we're entering into the relationship in good faith. Maybe that's what makes accepting a job like marriage. Even though you know it might not last, when you accept the relationship of working for a firm, you enter in good faith—fully intending at the time of your acceptance to abide by your commitment.

If I accepted Happy Co., but was really waiting for Manufacturco, it would be like Jeannette saying "Yes" to marrying me, when she really hoped Prince Charming would come along before our wedding day.

Gabrielle: I think you've being naïve, Hector. Since Happy Co. could dump you anytime they want, what makes you so committed to them?

Hector: Jeannette could "dump me" at any time, too. We don't have indentured marriage any more than we have indentured servitude. Does that mean that I could lie to her, cheat on her, dump her first?

David: But, Hector, let's say you wouldn't be happy at Happy Co. You have to act in your self-interest.

Hector: Keeping my self-respect is part of my self-interest.

This discussion in the Job Search Club highlighted for me the difficulty of the issues. Ethics and self-interest *often* come into conflict. Do we say "I've got to watch out for myself, no one else will?" Or do we say "If I'm concerned about myself *only,* what kind of person am I?"

I told the Job Search Club that I thought Hector's choice of ethics over self-interest was correct and that I hoped they would reach the same conclusion. Lauren immediately challenged me.

Lauren: Hector and you sound very high-minded. But let's be realistic. What kind of protection do we have if a firm rescinds an offer on us?

Richard: That's a fair question. Let's stick with the example of Hector and Happy Co. It is highly unlikely that Happy Co. would rescind its offer. First, Happy Co. may and should have ethical concerns. Second, it's not in the firm's pragmatic interest. It would damage its reputation at this college and others as well. In the case of Emeritus (and many other colleges), we would refuse to let Happy Co. use our placement facilities again.

Bill: That's great as a deterrent or as a punishment. But what if Happy Co. *does* rescind the offer to Hector? What happens *to him?*

Richard: If Happy Co. did rescind its offer, it might offer Hector some financial compensation. But, frankly, Happy Co. probably could not be compelled to do so.

To go back to our social analogy: It is possible, though unlikely, that Jeannette might leave Hector standing at the altar. Would that justify Hector's promising to marry a second woman as a hedge against what Jeannette might do?

Gabrielle: I know you think that not honoring a job acceptance is unethical. But let's say Hector *did* say "Yes" to Happy Co., and then reneged to accept a job with Manufacturco. Could Happy Co. take any legal action against Hector?

Richard: I am not a lawyer, so I won't speak from a legal perspective. However, it's not very likely that Happy Co. would take any legal action against Hector. It's hard to see what they would have to gain by doing so.

In this chapter, we saw how Robert went through the relatively objective Corporate Marriage Partner exercise and Alice used the totally subjective "good morning" test, to help evaluate their job offers. We also heard the Job Search Club debate ethics and saw how to avoid seeing a job choice as a decision between "the lady or the tiger."

In the next chapter, we will discuss "closing the loops." This is a critical, but sometimes overlooked, part of your job search process.

CHAPTER EIGHTEEN

Closing the Loops

In this chapter, I will show you how to accept and reject job offers, the importance of remembering your friends, and the benefit of writing your job search memoirs.

BE PROFESSIONAL WITH OFFERS

You worked hard on your résumé and interview skills. Your hard work resulted in some good job offers. You made your Follow-up Visits and evaluated each offer. You have decided which offer you're going to accept. Let's make sure you close the loops on your job search effort, for at least two reasons:

- *Ethics* — The Principles for Professional Conduct of the College Placement Council indicate that students have an ethical obligation to advise all those employers who have extended job offers of their accept/reject decision. The Principles codified an opinion generally shared by both college career professionals and corporate personnel.
- *Professional pragmatism* — Your good name is one of your strongest assets in building a career. Become known as a considerate person. First, don't leave those you're going to reject waiting for a response. Uncertainty complicates their hiring efforts. Second, thank *everyone* with whom you met during your job search process. They earned your thanks, and you don't want to become known as an ingrate. Whether for better or for worse, you never know when you'll run into the same people again.

ACCEPTING A JOB OFFER

If you haven't already given an oral acceptance at your Follow-up Visit (remember, many people do not), call the person who extended your offer.

Tell him or her that you are delighted with the offer and that you accept it. Indicate that you will send a written acceptance without delay. In your brief letter of acceptance, you should do at least the following:

- Thank the firm for your job offer;
- Review the basics: job title, starting date, location, and compensation terms;
- Express your excitement about starting your career at that firm;
- Indicate how and when any documents requested by the firm will be delivered.

As an example, look at Hector's acceptance letter to Manufacturco (Figure 18.1).

REJECTING A JOB OFFER

Once you have accepted a job offer, you should contact all other firms still considering you for employment and remove yourself from the process. The reasons are again related to ethics and professional pragmatism:

- *Ethics*—Employers need to know where they stand with students, just as you needed to know where you stood with prospective employers. By withdrawing from the process, you clarify the hiring picture for the employer and enable the firm to proceed more expeditiously with offers to other students.
- *Professional Pragmatism*—Firms do not like to have their time wasted or to look foolish pursuing a candidate who has already accepted a job. (It's like asking someone for a date who is already engaged.) Protect your reputation by advising each employer, by phone and brief letter, that you no longer wish to remain under consideration. Slighting people today may come back to haunt you tomorrow.

In your letter, be sure to say:

- Thank you for the offer of employment (*or*, for considering me for employment);
- I have decided to accept another offer;
- The firm's time and consideration are appreciated.

Figure 18.2 is an example of the letter Alice wrote when rejecting offers she had received.

If Alice had not yet received an offer from Sam Sanderson & Co. but was still under active consideration, her first line could have read:

Figure 18.1   Hector's letter of acceptance.

2468 Douglas Drive
Lincoln, NE 68529
March 20, 1993

Jim Flores
Vice President, Human Resources
Manufacturco
Widget Drive
San Diego, CA 92102

Dear Jim:

Thank you for your letter of March 15 in which you offered me employment with Manufacturco. As I indicated to you on the phone yesterday, I am excited about the offer and accept it.

To review the essence of your offer, I will start with Manufacturco's Financial Management Program in San Diego on July 1 of this year. My starting compensation will be $28,000 per year plus benefits. In addition, Manufacturco is extending me a one-time housing allowance of $600.

I am thrilled about the opportunity to build my career in finance at Manufacturco and I look forward to seeing you in July.

I have asked my college registrar to send you an *official* copy of my transcript as soon as possible. In the meantime, the most current copy of my unofficial transcript is enclosed.

Please let me know if you need any additional information from me.

Sincerely,

Hector Sanchez

Enclosure

As you and I discussed on the phone the other day, I am asking Sam Sanderson to remove me from further consideration for employment at this time.

or

After considerable thought, I am asking Sam Sanderson to remove me from further consideration for employment at this time.

Figure 18.2 Alice's letter of rejection.

9753 Pine Street
Lincoln, NE 68551
April 15, 1993

Mr. Louis Smith
Partner
Sam Sanderson & Co.
15 Cashin Street
Cedar Rapids, IA 52416

Dear Louis:

Thank you for your letter of January 15, offering me employment with Sam Sanderson & Co.

It has been a difficult decision, but I have determined to begin my career with another firm.

The time and consideration given me by you and so many people at Sam Sanderson are deeply appreciated.

Sincerely,

Alice Perugia

REMEMBERING YOUR CONTACTS

If you followed my advice throughout this book, you will have sought and received help from many individuals in the course of your job search. For example, remember how Aunt Millie helped David by putting him in touch with her friend Sheila? Now that David has accepted a job, he should contact both Aunt Millie and Sheila, to thank them and keep them abreast of his job situation. Presumably, David can just pick up the phone and call his aunt. For Sheila, a quick note like the one shown in Figure 18.3 may be more appropriate.

There are two reasons for David (and you) to thank those who were helpful in the job search:

- *Courtesy*—it never goes out of season;
- *Professional pragmatism*—if you stay in touch with people when you don't want something from them, they are more likely to be helpful when you *do* need something.

Figure 18.3   David's thank-you note.

Dear Sheila:

I want to thank you again for the information and advice you shared with me when we met last October. Your insights and suggestions were helpful to me as I pursued a job in sales.

Due in part to your help, I was offered a wonderful sales position with General Thrills, starting in July. I'll keep you posted as my career develops.

Sincerely,

David Peters

One of the things David is doing with his thank-you letters is preserving a network of professional friends he may need as his career progresses.

WRITING YOUR MEMOIRS

Usually, when we think of someone writing his or her memoirs, we picture a senior citizen, at the close of a career, looking back over a fruitful life. I suggest that you write your job search memoirs before your career actually begins. They will be a resource to make your next job search easier, and you may need a list for "moments like these."

A Resource for Next Time

Your memoirs should include

- The name, professional affiliation, and phone number of *everyone* whom you met with during your job search. Include your informational meetings, interviews, and Site Visits, even if the firm did not extend you an offer.
- Save your SSP, your various charts (twin peaks, research), and copies of your letters. Some of the information they contain may be directly helpful in the future. At a minimum, they will help you see how you've changed or grown when you look back on them.
- Outline the steps you took in your job search; you may be taking similar steps in the future.

A List for "Moments Like These"

Most people experience a period of unhappiness on a job. The workload becomes too heavy; compensation is less than a friend's; the boss is a grouch; the commute is too long; someone else got a coveted promotion; the weather is lousy. At times like these, it's easier to bear up under the strain if you have a list detailing the reasons you chose to come to that employer in the first place. When you ask yourself "What Am I Doing Here?," your List of Positive Reasons for wanting the job will help counterbalance the negative experiences you're going through.

I am not suggesting that you stay with any given job forever. I am saying that you should try to see your job in a reasonable perspective, and your List of Positive Reasons can be very helpful.

A Job and Marriage

Throughout this book, I have drawn an analogy between the job search process and social relations. We said, for example, that a job offer is like an offer of marriage.

I am not a marriage counselor, but I am a happily married man. Let me give you this piece of unsolicited, nonprofessional advice.

Before your wedding, while you're still aglow with romance, write a Love List of all the good reasons why you love and are marrying your Significant Other. Then, if you go through a time when everything seems to be going wrong, pull out your Love List. By reminding yourself of the positives in your relationship, you'll put things in a more realistic perspective—a good remedy for keeping your marriage healthy and alive.

In this chapter, you learned about ethical and pragmatic reasons for closing the loops and exactly how to close them. You also learned why it's helpful to write your job search memoirs.

The next chapter is for you to write. Perhaps you'll call it "The Beginning of My Glorious Career."

I would love to hear from you—how you have used this book, how your job search progresses, and where you start your career. You can write to me at the School of Management, University of Massachusetts, Amherst, MA 01003. Good luck!

Useful Sources

FOR YOUR INTERVIEW PREPARATION

Business Newsbank—Full text (on microfiche) of business articles in regional journals and newspapers from over 450 U.S. cities. Index has two sections: geographical (state and city) and industry/product/company name.

Encyclopedia of Business Information Sources—Handbooks and manuals, directories, periodicals, general works, trade associations, and databases for specific industries.

InfoTrac—Index to periodical articles in business and trade journals, general interest magazines, and general social science journals; updated monthly. Library of Congress subject headings are used. Menu drive is user-friendly.

Standard & Poor's Industry Surveys—A quarterly publication covering about 70 industries; summarizes current information about an industry and indicates trends.

Survey of Current Business—monthly publication of the U.S. Department of Commerce. Data are for general business and leading economic indictors. Each issue includes some industry analysis.

U.S. Industrial Outlook—An annual publication by the U.S. Department of Commerce; indicates trends for over 300 different industries.

BOOKS FOR YOUR OUTREACH EFFORT

American Export Register—good for identifying U.S. exporters and importers; banks, American chambers of commerce in foreign countries; services and institutions concerned with foreign trade.

America's Corporate Families: The Billion-Dollar Directory, Vols. 1 and 2— great for identifying American corporations and their domestic divisions and subsidiaries; lists overseas affiliates and subsidiaries of U.S. firms.

Corporate Finance Sourcebook—a reference-library guide to leading firms in corporate financing, including venture capital firms, investment banks, accounting firms, and security analysts.

Directory of Department Stores (annual)—includes information about 900 department store companies and indicates sales volume, store locations, and key executives; 950 mail order firms are also included.

Directory of Leading U.S. Export Management Companies, 3rd Edition.

Emerson's Directory of Leading U.S. Accounting Firms, 2nd Edition—data on 3,500 American CPA firms.

Hoover's Handbook—profiles of over 500 major corporations; useful information for both outreach campaign and interview preparation. Consider purchasing this book.

Macmillan Directory of Leading Private Companies—a leading reference to large *privately held* companies in the United States.

The 100 Best Companies to Sell For—a good picture of what it's like to work for these firms; offers a mailing list.

Security Dealers of North America—lists thousands of brokerage and investment houses.

Standard Directory of Advertisers ("the Red Book")—contains names of over 25,000 firms that advertise—not advertising agencies; useful to identify firms in various fields.

ADDITIONAL REFERENCES

Accounting Firms and Practitioners (AICPA)
Consultants and Consulting Organizations Directory
International Directory of Marketing Research Houses and Services
Polk's World Banking Directory
Standard Directory of Advertising Agencies

Index